C(

INTRODUCTION
VEGETABLE AND SIDE DISHES RECIPES
   1. Brined Olives And Fresh Tomatoes In Couscous
   2. Healthy Potato Salad
   3. Snow Peas With Bell Peppers
   4. Rice Cooker Polenta
   5. Tofu Vegetable Delight
   6. Spicy Sprouts Pilaf
   7. Tuna Tomato Tabouleh
   8. Mesmerizing Romano Cheese Pasta
   9. Simplest Potato Salad Ever
   10. Subtle "yellow" Dal
   11. Broccoli And Cauliflower Couscous
   12. Quinoa Pomegranate Salad
   13. Deliciously Steamed Mac And Cheese
   14. Healthy Kale Pasta
   15. Hearty Squash Delight
   16. Potatoes Kale Mix
POULTRY, BEEF, SEAFOOD AND PORK
   17. Juicy Chicken Paella
   18. Delicious Pulled Pork Bbq Loafers
   19. Rustic Meatballs Spaghettis
   20. Chicken With Vegetables
   21. Holy Shrimp Jambalaya
   22. California Turkey And Avocado Salad
   23. Dijon Chicken Mushroom Platter
   24. Simple Yet Efficient Chicken Chili
   25. Fish Tacos With Sesame Sauce
   26. Efficient Paprika Chicken
   27. Classic Balsamic Chicken
   28. Beef And Cabbage Roll
   29. Meatballs From Sweden
   30. Beautiful Curried Squash And Pork
   31. Delicious Whole Chicken
SOUPS, STEWS AND CHILIES
   32. A Fine Taco Soup

33. Authentic Tortellini Soup
34. Fascinating Rice Chili Stew
35. A Fine Vegetable Stew
36. Tantalizing Split Pea Soup
37. Pork And Mushroom Creamy Stew
38. Healthy Veggie Lentil Soup
39. Spicy Lemongrass Shrimp Bowl
40. Lentils Kale Miso Soup
41. Coolest Rice Beef Soup
42. Chicken White Radish Soup
43. Extra Creamy Mushroom Soup
44. Grand Ma's Chicken Soup
45. Very Comforting Beef Stew
46. Exquisite Clam Chowder
47. Pork And Vegetable Spicy Stew

RICE AND OTHER GRAINS

48. Authentic Thai Chicken Rice
49. Spicy Cajun Crawfish Tails With Rice
50. "pirates Of The Caribbean" Rice
51. Very "wild" Rice
52. Beautiful Lemon Rice
53. Amazing Ginger And Chicken Rice
54. Traditional Basmati Rice
55. Creamy Chicken Mushroom Rice
56. Hearty Bacon Rice
57. Authentic Spanish Rice
58. Chicken And Ginger Rice Meal
59. Sesame Chicken Rice
60. Rocking And Flying Risotto
61. Delicious Saffron Yellow Rice With Fruit Chutney
62. Brown Rice Tabbouleh
63. Peanut Butter Rice
64. Berryful Goldilocks Porridge
65. Cashew And Cherry Rice
66. Healthy Mexican Green Rice
67. Jasmine Rice Pilaf
68. Vegetables Rice

69. Exciting Shrimp And Quail Eggs With Java Rice
70. Bacon Mushroom Risotto
71. Simple Salmon And Rice Delight
72. Original Moroccan Brown Rice
73. Sweet Corn And Wild Rice
74. Dill And Lemon "feta" Rice
75. Rice And Chinese Sausage
76. Chicken Biryani And Saffron Cream
77. Thai Prawn With Peas Fried Rice
78. Red Ruby Beans And Rice
79. Fine Chile Cheese Rice
80. Mesmerizing Garlic And Chicken Fragrant Rice
81. Ultimate Orange Chipotle Risotto
82. Mouthwatering Curry Chicken Jambalaya
83. Bacon And Onion Rice
84. Dirty Rice And Chinese Chorizo
85. Curious Red Rice
86. Shiitake Black Bean Rice
87. Simplest Tomato Rice
88. Spicy Cajun Wild Rice
89. Easy To Make Lime Cilantro Dish
90. Peanut Rice And Bell Pepper
91. Fragrant Basmati Rice
92. Sweet Ginger Porridge
93. Almonds Corn Quinoa
94. Southwestern Rice Cooker Quinoa Yum
95. Sensible Mirin Rice
96. Toasted Coconut Yellow Rice
97. Simplest Curry Rice Ever
98. Fuss Free Simple Risotto
99. Generic Brown Rice
100. Coconut Rice And Roasted Almonds

INTRODUCTION

Hamilton Beach Rice Cooker

Make mounds of delicious, fluffy rice with minimal effort.

Making rice and whole grains in the Hamilton Beach Rice Cooker & Steamer is as easy as placing the ingredients in the nonstick bowl and turning it on. The rice will cook perfectly on its own, giving you time to prepare the rest of your meal. There's no need to worry about boiling water, adjusting the temperature or even setting a timer - it will automatically shift to warm once the cook cycle is complete. And with a 16 cup cooked rice capacity, you'll have enough to feed a crowd.

Use the included 2-in-1 basket to rinse rice or grains ahead of cooking, or use it to steam everything from salmon to zucchini. Clean up is a snap with the dishwasher safe nonstick cooking bowl and rice rinser/steam basket. The lid liner can also be removed for quick cleaning.

16 cup cooked rice capacity, 8 cup uncooked
Included rice rinser doubles as a steam basket
Cook rice, whole grains, hot cereal, steamed vegetables & much more
Automatically cooks rice, then shifts to warm
Steam food while rice cooks below
Dishwasher safe nonstick pot and glass lid
Dishwasher safe nonstick bowl and glass lid
Dishwasher safe rice rinser/steam basket, rice paddle & measuring cup
Perfect rice every time - Automatically cooks up to 16 cups of rice, then shifts to keep warm

VEGETABLE AND SIDE DISHES RECIPES

1. Brined Olives And Fresh Tomatoes In Couscous

Servings: 4
Cooking Time: 45 Minutes
Ingredients:

- 1 small lime, sliced into wedges remove pips for garnish
- Salad
- 2 garlic cloves, minced
- 1 small lime, juiced (reserve 1 tablespoon for garnish)
- 1 pound ripe cherry tomatoes, quartered
- 1 pound unripe cherry tomatoes, quartered
- ¼ teaspoon agave sugar, crumbled
- 1 teaspoon olive oil
- Salt and pepper to taste
- For Couscous
- 2 cups pearl couscous
- ½ cup Kalamata olive in brine, drained and pitted, roughly chopped
- 1 cup mushroom broth
- ½ cup mint, minced
- ¼ cup fresh parsley, minced
- 1 teaspoon fresh thyme, minced
- Salt and pepper to taste

Directions:

1. Take a bowl and whisk lime juice and sugar together.
2. Add the rest of the salad ingredients to the bowl and pour seasoned lime juice on top Give it a good stir and refrigerate.
3. Next, add in the couscous and olives in your Hamilton Beach Cooker. Pour broth to line 4. Close the lid, press BROWN RICE, and let the cycle complete.
4. Once it goes off, the cooker will automatically switch to WARM mode.
5. Open the lid and add the rest of the ingredients. Stir well.
6. Adjust seasoning and serve ladling 1 portion couscous into 1 portion

tomato salad. Garnish with fresh parsley and lemon wedge, enjoy with a squeeze fresh juice!

Nutrition Info: Calories: 368 Fat: 9g Carbohydrates: 63g Protein: 10g

2. Healthy Potato Salad

Servings: 6
Cooking Time: 20 Minutes
Ingredients:

- 1 pound new potatoes, cut into bite-sized portions
- 1 pound fresh green beans, trimmed and cut in half
- ½ medium red onion, chopped
- ½ cup Kalamata olives, pitted
- 1 tablespoon Dijon mustard
- 2 cups water
- ¼ cup extra virgin olive oil
- Salt and Pepper to taste

Directions:

1. Pour water to line 2. Add the potatoes and season with salt and pepper.
2. Close the lid, push the STEAM button, and set the timer to 10 minutes.
3. Once it goes off, carefully open the lid and add the green beans. Push the STEAM button and cook for 10 minutes.
4. Serve by placing potatoes and beans in a serving bowl and top with red onion and olives. Take a bowl and whisk mustard and oil, season with salt and pepper. Pour the dressing over the vegetables and serve warm.

Nutrition Info: Calories: 217 Fat: 15g Carbohydrates: 19g Protein: 2g

3. Snow Peas With Bell Peppers

Servings: 4

Cooking Time: 15 Minutes
Ingredients:

- 1 tablespoon olive oil
- 4 shiitake mushrooms, cut in half
- 1 red bell pepper, seeded and sliced
- 1 garlic, minced
- 3 tablespoons water
- 8 ounces snow peas
- Salt and pepper to taste

Directions:

1. Push the STEAM cook and set timer for 15 minutes.
2. Pour oil and heat it. Stir in garlic and cook for 1 minute or until fragrant.
3. Add in the mushrooms and cook for 3 minutes. Then, add the snow peas and add water to line 2. Cook for 3 more minutes.
4. Next, add the bell pepper and mix well. Cook for 5 additional minutes.
5. Season with salt and pepper, and serve.

Nutrition Info: Calories: 94 Fat: 5g Carbohydrates: 20g Protein: 4g

4. Rice Cooker Polenta

Servings: 4
Cooking Time: 20 Minutes
Ingredients:

- 1 cup cornmeal
- 3 cups water
- ¼ cup parmesan cheese, grated
- 3 green onions, finely chopped
- 1 tablespoon olive oil
- ½ teaspoon oregano
- ½ teaspoon basil
- ½ teaspoon thyme

- ¼ teaspoon marjoram
- ¼ teaspoon sage

Directions:

1. Add all the ingredients to your Hamilton Beach Rice Cooker, except for parmesan cheese. Close the lid, press the WHITE RICE button, and let the cycle complete.
2. Once the cooker switches to WARM mode, let it sit for 10 minutes, lid closed.
3. Sprinkle with freshly grated parmesan cheese and serve hot!

Nutrition Info: Calories: 294 Fat: 14g Carbohydrates: 32g Protein: 10g

5. Tofu Vegetable Delight

Servings: 4
Cooking Time: 20 Minutes
Ingredients:

- 6 ounces firm tofu, cut into cubes
- 2 tablespoons oyster sauce
- 1 teaspoon toasted sesame oil
- 1 teaspoon vegetable oil
- 1 teaspoon honey
- 1 tablespoon soy sauce
- 1 garlic clove, minced
- ½ bunch asparagus, trimmed and cut into ½ inch slices
- 1 carrot, peeled into matchsticks

Directions:

1. Take a bowl and mix in the seasoning.
2. Add the rest the ingredients and toss well.
3. Transfer the mixture to a heatproof bowl.
4. Place the bowl to your Hamilton Beach cooker and pour enough water to surround the bowl.
5. Close the lid, push the STEAM button, and set the timer to 20

minutes.
6. Carefully open the lid and serve hot.

Nutrition Info: Calories: 279 Fat: 19g Carbohydrates: 14g Protein: 18g

6. Spicy Sprouts Pilaf

Servings: 4
Cooking Time: 30 Minutes
Ingredients:

- 1 cup soaked basmati rice
- 1 cup bean sprouts
- 1 tablespoon ginger-garlic paste
- 1 onion, finely chopped
- 2 small red chilies
- 1 bay leaf
- 2 cloves garlic
- ¾ tablespoon salt
- 2 cups water
- 1 teaspoon coconut oil

Directions:

1. Push the STEAM button and set the timer to 5 minutes.
2. Add the oil and heat it.
3. Next, stir in the ginger-garlic paste, red chilies, onion, bay leaf and cloves. Sauté them for 4-5 minutes.
4. Then, add in the rest the ingredients.
5. Close the lid and press WHITE RICE and let it cook until the cycle completes.
6. Once the cooker switches to WARM mode, let it sit for 5 minutes.
7. Fluff with a fork and serve!

Nutrition Info: Calories: 251 Fat: 7g Carbohydrates: 39g Protein: 7g

7. Tuna Tomato Tabouleh

Servings: 4
Cooking Time: 22 Minutes
Ingredients:

- 1 cup bulgur wheat, uncooked
- ½ pound fresh tuna steak
- 1 cup small grape tomatoes, halved
- 1 medium cucumber, peeled and diced
- ¼ cup Italian dressing
- 2 cups water
- Salt and pepper to taste

Directions:

1. Pour water to line 2 in your pressure cooker.
2. Add the bulgur wheat.
3. Season with a pinch of salt and pepper.
4. Close the lid, push the STEAM button, and set the timer to 17 minutes.
5. Place tuna on a steam tray.
6. Once cooking is complete, open the lid and place the steam tray inside.
7. STEAM cook for 5 more minutes.
8. Open the lid and remove the tuna, set aside.
9. Allow the Bulgur to cool.
10. Transfer the cooled bulgur to serving bowls and add tomatoes and cucumber.
11. Sprinkle with Italian seasoning.
12. Slice the tuna steak thinly and place on top of the salad.

Nutrition Info: Calories: 460 Fat: 26g Carbohydrates: 31g Protein: 28g

8. Mesmerizing Romano Cheese Pasta

Servings: 4
Cooking Time: 25 Minutes
Ingredients:

- 2 cups water
- 1 cup tomato sauce
- ¼ cup cooked ground beef
- ¼ teaspoon salt
- 1 teaspoon olive oil
- ¼ teaspoon dried oregano
- ¼ cup Romano cheese, grated
- 2 cups uncooked rigatoni pasta

Directions:

1. Add all the ingredients to your Hamilton Beach Cooker, except for the oregano and the cheese.
2. Stir well and season with salt.
3. Close the lid and, press WHITE RICE, and allow the cycle to complete.
4. Once it goes off, the cooker will automatically switch to WARM mode.
5. Carefully open the lid, sprinkle with the grated romano cheese and the dried oregano.
6. Let it sit on WARM mode for 2-3 minutes until the cheese melts and serve immediately.

Nutrition Info: Calories: 333 Fat: 9g Carbohydrates: 51g Protein: 13g

9. Simplest Potato Salad Ever

Servings: 4
Cooking Time: 15 Minutes
Ingredients:

- 1 ½ pound small potatoes
- 1 ½ cups water
- 1 ½ cups mayonnaise
- 1 tablespoon extra virgin olive oil
- 1 ½ tablespoons vinegar
- 1 teaspoon celery seeds
- 2 tablespoons chopped onions

- 2 stalks celery, chopped
- 2 teaspoons prepared mustard
- 1 ½ tablespoons pickled relish
- ½ teaspoon salt
- 4 hardboiled eggs, coarsely chopped

Directions:

1. Cut the potatoes into bite-sized pieces and add them to your Hamilton Beach Cooker.
2. Add water and close the lid.
3. Press STEAM and cook for 12-15 minutes until the potatoes are cooked (tender).
4. Take the rice cooker pan to the sink and run cold water onto the potatoes and eggs, cool them and drain them.
5. Take a bowl and add the potatoes and the eggs.
6. Add the rest the ingredients and toss well.
7. Refrigerate for a while and serve cold.

Nutrition Info: Calories: 217 Fat: 15g Carbohydrates: 19g Protein: 2g

10. Subtle "yellow" Dal

Servings: 4
Cooking Time: 20 Minutes
Ingredients:

- 1 cup chickpea dal
- 1 onion, finely chopped
- 1 onion, thinly sliced
- 4 garlic cloves, minced
- 1 teaspoon cumin powder
- 2 mild green chilies
- 1 teaspoon tamarind paste
- 1 teaspoon olive oil
- 2 cups water

Directions:

1. Push the STEAM button and set timer to 10 minutes. Add oil and heat it.
2. Stir in the ginger, garlic, chilies and onion and sauté for 2-3 minutes.
3. Then, add the remaining ingredients and close the lid Select WHITE RICE and let the cooking cycle to complete.
4. Once it goes off, it will automatically switch to WARM mode. Open the lid and check consistency. Let it sit on WARM for 5 minutes before serving.

Nutrition Info: Calories: 326 Fat: 10g Carbohydrates: 49g Protein: 14g

11. Broccoli And Cauliflower Couscous

Servings: 6
Cooking Time: 45-55 Minutes
Ingredients:

- For Steamed Vegetables
- 1 head, small broccoli, sliced into florets, rinsed and drained
- 1 head, small cauliflower, sliced into florets, drained
- Garlic salt
- For Couscous
- 2 cups pearl couscous
- 1 piece, small shallot, minced
- 1 teaspoon olive oil
- ½ teaspoon kosher salt
- ¼ teaspoon smoked paprika
- 1 cup mushroom broth
- For garnish
- 1 teaspoon fresh parsley, minced
- 1 piece, small lime, sliced into wedges

Directions:

1. Add cauliflower and broccoli to your steamer tray.
2. Heat oil in a skillet over medium heat. Add in the couscous and sauté until lightly toasted and coated with oil. Transfer to your Hamilton Beach Cooker.

3. Add the rest of the ingredients listed under couscous. Give it a good stir.
4. Pour the broth to line 4, and place the steamer tray on top.
5. Close the lid, push BROWN RICE and let the cycle complete.
6. Once ready, the cooker will automatically switch to WARM.
7. Carefully remove the lid and drain the vegetables.
8. Season with a dash of garlic salt, and serve the couscous with veggies.

Nutrition Info: Calories: 189 Fat: 5g Carbohydrates: 31g Protein: 6g

12. Quinoa Pomegranate Salad

Servings: 4
Cooking Time: 35 Minutes
Ingredients:

- 2 cups quinoa, rinsed
- 4 cups water
- 1 cup pomegranate seeds
- ½ teaspoon all-spice powder
- ½ cup fresh mint, chopped
- 1 tablespoon pine nuts, toasted
- Juice from 1 lemon
- 1 teaspoon olive oil
- Salt and pepper to taste

Directions:

1. Add quinoa, water and a pinch of salt to your Hamilton Beach Cooker. Close the lid, press BROWN RICE, and let the cycle complete.
2. In the meantime, toast the pine nuts over medium heat in a skillet.
3. Once the quinoa is ready, carefully open the lid and add the spice powder and lemon juice. Give it a good stir and let cool.
4. Once cooled, add the pomegranate seeds and pine nuts. Toss and serve!

Nutrition Info: Calories: 350 Fat: 17g Carbohydrates: 40g Protein: 12g

13. Deliciously Steamed Mac And Cheese

Servings: 3
Cooking Time: 40 Minutes
Ingredients:

- 1 ½ cups elbow macaroni
- 1 ½ cups vegetable broth
- 1 cup unsweetened almond milk
- ¾ cup cheddar cheese, shredded
- ½ cup mozzarella cheese, shredded
- ¼ cup parmesan cheese, grated
- ¼ teaspoon paprika
- Salt and pepper to taste

Directions:

1. Add macaroni, broth, almond milk to your Hamilton Beach Cooker. Push the STEAM button and set to 40 minutes. Seal the lid and cook until the macaroni are tender.
2. Open the lid and stir in the cheeses, salt, paprika and pepper. Give it a good stir.
3. Let steam until the cheese melts. Serve immediately and enjoy.

Nutrition Info: Calories: 522 Fat: 24g Carbohydrates: 51g Protein: 25g

14. Healthy Kale Pasta

Servings: 4
Cooking Time: 15 Minutes
Ingredients:

- 1 ½ cups kale, chopped
- 1 ½ cups whole wheat pasta
- ½ cup kidney beans, cooked
- 3 garlic cloves, minced
- 1 onion, finely chopped
- 1 teaspoon oregano
- ½ teaspoon thyme

- Salt and pepper to taste
- 2 ½ cups water

Directions:

1. Add all the above listed ingredients to your Hamilton Beach cooker. Stir well and seal the lid. Push the STEAM button and set the timer to 15 minutes.
2. Carefully open the lid, give it a good stir and serve immediately.

Nutrition Info: Calories: 242 Fat: 9g Carbohydrates: 31g Protein: 9g

15. Hearty Squash Delight

Servings: 2
Cooking Time: 20 Minutes
Ingredients:

- 1 pound small acorn squash, cut into bite-sized portions
- 1 tablespoon fresh sage
- 2 tablespoons butter
- 2 cups water
- Salt and Pepper to taste

Directions:

1. Add water to line 2. Spoon Acorn Squash into the steam tray, and sprinkle with sage.
2. Place the steam tray into your Rice Cooker and close the lid.
3. Push the STEAM button, set the timer to 20 minutes, and let the cycle complete.
4. Spoon the cooked squash into serving bowls, add a bit butter, salt and pepper.

Nutrition Info: Calories: 125 Fat: 7g Carbohydrates: 10g Protein: 6g

16. Potatoes Kale Mix

Servings: 6

Cooking Time: 35 Minutes

Ingredients:

- 1 cup couscous
- 2 golden potatoes, diced
- 9-10 kale leaves, chopped
- 1 cup vegetable stock
- 1 teaspoon cumin
- 1 ½ tablespoon lemon juice
- ½ teaspoon lemon zest
- 1 teaspoon parsley
- ¾ tablespoon salt
- ½ teaspoon coconut oil

Directions:

1. Push the STEAM button and set timer to 40 minutes. Add oil and heat it. Add in the potatoes, couscous, cumin and kale leaves.
2. Sauté for 4-5 minutes. Then, add the rest the ingredients and close the lid.
3. Let them cook for 30-35 minutes. Once the cooking is complete, carefully open the lid stir and serve immediately.

Nutrition Info: Calories: 548 Fat: 34g Carbohydrates: 38g Protein: 27g

POULTRY, BEEF, SEAFOOD AND PORK

17. Juicy Chicken Paella

Servings: 4
Cooking Time: 55 Minutes
Ingredients:

- 1 ½ cups basmati rice
- 4 cups chicken stock
- ¾ pound skinless and boneless chicken breast
- ¼ pound shrimps, peeled, deveined and chopped
- ¼ chopped brown onion
- 1 cup water
- 3 ounces green chilies
- 6 ounces unsalted tomato sauce
- 1 tomato , diced
- 1 tablespoon olive oil
- ¾ teaspoon ground cumin
- 4 teaspoons chili powder
- ¼ teaspoon smoked paprika

Directions:

1. Coat the rice cooker with olive oil.
2. Add all the ingredients in the order given above.
3. Stir gently, then close the lid.
4. Press the BROWN RICE button and let the cooking cycle complete.
5. When ready, the cooker will switch to WARM mode.
6. Carefully open the lid and serve hot.

Nutrition Info: Calories: 585 Fat: 33g Carbohydrates: 50g Protein: 32g

18. Delicious Pulled Pork Bbq Loafers

Servings: 4
Cooking Time: 30 Minutes
Ingredients:

- 10-12 ounces pork tenderloins
- 1 cup BBQ sauce
- 1 cup chili sauce
- 1 white onion, peeled and chopped
- 4-6 soft, hefty sandwich buns, split and toasted
- 2 ½ cups water

Directions:

1. Cover steam tray with 2 sheets of aluminum foil.
2. Place the tenderloins on the tray.
3. Top the pork with BBQ sauce and chili sauce. Scatter onions on top.
4. Pour water into your pot to line 2 and close the lid.
5. Press the STEAM button and set timer to 25-30 minutes.
6. Check the internal temperature using a thermometer, it should read 160° F.
7. Once the meat is tender, take it out and place on a cutting board.
8. Shred using a fork and mix with the remaining sauce.
9. To serve, mount on or between sandwich buns.

Nutrition Info: Calories: 501 Fat: 32g Carbohydrates: 4g Protein: 46g

19. Rustic Meatballs Spaghettis

Servings: 4
Cooking Time: 30 Minutes
Ingredients:

- 1 jar marinara sauce
- 3 ½ cups water
- ½ pound spaghetti
- 1 pound meatballs
- 2 large cloves garlic, minced
- 2 tablespoons parsley, chopped
- 1 teaspoon Italian herbs

Directions:

1. Take a bowl and add all the listed ingredients. Mix them well and transfer them to your Hamilton Beach Cooker.
2. Push the STEAM button and set timer to 20 minutes.
3. Close the lid and let the cooking cycle complete. Once done, open the lid and stir well. Serve and enjoy!

Nutrition Info: Calories: 476 Fat: 20g Carbohydrates: 63g Protein: 13g

20. Chicken With Vegetables

Servings: 4
Cooking Time: 45-50 Minutes
Ingredients:

- 10 ounce skinless and boneless chicken breast, cut into ½ inch cubes
- 1 cup white rice
- 2 cups vegetable stock
- ½ cup broccoli, cut into florets
- ½ cup green beans, cut into ½ inch pieces
- 1 teaspoon oregano, chopped
- 1 teaspoon thyme, chopped
- 2 teaspoons vegetable oil
- ¼ teaspoon cayenne pepper
- Salt and pepper to taste

Directions:

1. Press the WHITE RICE button on your Hamilton Beach Rice Cooker.
2. Heat the oil and add the chicken.
3. Cook the chicken for 4-5 minute until slightly browned.
4. Add the rest of the ingredients and stir gently.
5. Close the lid and cook until the cycle completes and the rice is tender.
6. Once ready, carefully open the lid and serve hot.

Nutrition Info: Calories: 309 Fat: 18g Carbohydrates: 19g Protein: 17g

21. Holy Shrimp Jambalaya

Servings: 6
Cooking Time: 75 Minutes
Ingredients:

- 2 cups brown rice
- 1 pound shrimp, peeled and deveined
- 1 can (14.5 ounce) chicken broth
- 1 can (10 ounce) tomato sauce
- 1 bell pepper, minced
- ½ cup butter
- 1 jar mushrooms, undrained

Directions:

1. Add the rice, shrimp, chicken broth, bell pepper, tomato sauce, mushrooms and butter to your Hamilton Beach Cooker.
2. Close the lid, push the STEAM button, and set timer to 75 minutes.
3. Let the cooking cycle complete but make sure to open the lid every 25 minutes and give it a gentle stir.
4. Once the cooking is over, carefully open the lid and serve immediately!

Nutrition Info: Calories: 369 Fat: 24g Carbohydrates: 12g Protein: 27g

22. California Turkey And Avocado Salad

Servings: 4
Cooking Time: 12 Minutes
Ingredients:

- 3 large eggs
- 12 ounces turkey cutlets
- 3 ripe avocados, peeled and sliced
- 8 cups assorted salad greens
- ¾ cup blue cheese salad dressing
- 2 cups water
- Salt and pepper to taste

Directions:

1. Add water to line 2. Place the unshelled eggs and turkey cutlets in the steamer tray. Season with salt and pepper.
2. Place the tray in your Hamilton Beach Cooker and close the lid. Press the STEAM button and set the timer to 12 minutes.
3. Remove the eggs and transfer to a bowl with cold water. Peel and cut them into wedges. Cut the cooked turkey cutlets into matchstick pieces.
4. To assemble, take a salad bowl and add greens, top them with turkey, eggs and sliced avocados. Sprinkle with blue cheese dressing and enjoy.

Nutrition Info: Calories: 482 Fat: 22g Carbohydrates: 36g Protein: 37g

23. Dijon Chicken Mushroom Platter

Servings: 4
Cooking Time: 30 Minutes
Ingredients:

- ¼ cup parsley, minced
- 1 ½ cups vegetable broth
- 1 cup farro
- 8 ounces crimini mushroom, quartered
- 2 shallots, minced
- 1 teaspoon olive oil
- 4 pieces of 5 ounces chicken breast, skinless and boneless
- 2 cups chicken broth
- For Marinade
- 1 tablespoon mustard, Dijon
- 1 teaspoon olive oil
- ⅓ cup balsamic vinegar
- Salt and pepper to taste

Directions:

1. Make the marinade by mixing all the ingredients listed under marinade in a zip bag. Add the chicken and coat it well. Refrigerate it for 2 hours.

2. Wait for 2 hours and then press the STEAM button on your rice cooker.
3. Set the timer to 90 minutes. Add oil and heat it. Stir in the shallots and close the lid.
4. Cook for 5 minutes until the shallots become tender. Carefully open the lid and add in the mushrooms. Cook for 8 more minutes, lid closed.
5. Once ready, open the lid, stir in the farro and cook for 3 minutes.
6. Add broth to line 2 and stir. Take the chicken out of the bag and place it inside the cooker. Discard the marinade.
7. Close the lid and let the STEAM cycle to complete.
8. Once it goes off, carefully open the lid.
9. To serve, place the mushroom and farro mix on a plate, and top with the chicken. Sprinkle with parsley and enjoy.

Nutrition Info: Calories: 301 Fat: 26g Carbohydrates: 2g Protein: 14g

24. Simple Yet Efficient Chicken Chili

Servings: 4
Cooking Time: 40 Minutes
Ingredients:

- 14 ounce can kidney beans, drained and rinsed
- 1 pound ground chicken
- 1 tablespoon tomato paste
- 1 can black beans, drained and rinsed
- 1 tablespoon chili powder
- 2 teaspoons dried oregano
- 1 cup tomato sauce
- 1 tablespoon vegetable oil
- Salt and pepper to taste

Directions:

1. Press the STEAM button and set timer to 40 minutes.
2. Heat the oil, add the chicken pieces and cook for 7-10 minutes until slightly browned.
3. Stir in the beans, tomato paste, sauce and spices.

4. Close the lid and cook for 30 minutes.
5. Once cooked, carefully open the lid and serve immediately.

Nutrition Info: Calories: 258 Fat: 9g Carbohydrates: 16g Protein: 28g

25. Fish Tacos With Sesame Sauce

Servings: 4
Cooking Time: 15 Minutes
Ingredients:

- 2 cups chicken broth
- 1 pound mild, white fish fillets
- ¾ cup sesame salad dressing
- 3 cups Asian Cole Slaw salad mix
- 12 small corn tortillas, warm
- Salt and pepper to taste

Directions:

1. Pour chicken broth to line 2 and add the fish to the steamer tray. Season with salt and pepper, and place the steamer tray in the Hamilton Beach cooker.
2. Close the lid and push the STEAM button. Set the timer to 15 minutes and let the cooking cycle complete.
3. Once completed, remove the fish and cut into bite-sized portions. Toss the fish with ¼ cup your salad dressing.
4. Fill each corn tortilla with fish and Cole Slaw. Drizzle more sauce and serve!

Nutrition Info: Calories: 320 Fat: 17g Carbohydrates: 10g Protein: 33g

26. Efficient Paprika Chicken

Servings: 6
Cooking Time: 55 Minutes
Ingredients:

- 3 tablespoons all-purpose flour

- 2 pounds chicken breast, cut into ½ inch strips
- 2 cups chopped onion
- 1 ¼ cups chicken broth
- 2 tablespoons sweet paprika
- 2 teaspoons minced garlic
- 1 teaspoon salt
- 1 pack pre-sliced mushrooms (8 ounce)
- 1 ¼ cups sour cream
- 2 tablespoons olive oil

Directions:

1. Push the STEAM button and set timer to 60 minutes. Add the oil and heat it.
2. Stir in onions and cook them for 3 minutes or until translucent.
3. Meanwhile, take a bowl and add flour and chicken. Toss well.
4. Add the chicken to the cooker and cook until brown, for about 4-5 minutes.
5. Add the next 6 ingredients, except for the sour cream and close the lid.
6. Let the STEAM cook cycle complete and wait until it switches to WARM mode. Carefully open the lid and add the sour cream.
7. Give it a good stir and let it heat for a few minutes.
8. Serve hot.

Nutrition Info: Calories: 265 Fat: 11g Carbohydrates: 11g Protein: 27g

27. Classic Balsamic Chicken

Servings: 4
Cooking Time: 1 Hour 20 Minutes
Ingredients:

- 4 pieces of 6 ounces skinless and boneless chicken breast
- 8 ounces quartered white mushrooms
- 4 tablespoons chopped parsley
- 2 shallots, minced
- 1 teaspoon olive oil

- 1 ½ cups chicken stock
- ½ cup balsamic vinegar
- 2 tablespoons mustard
- 1 cup farro

Directions:

1. Mix balsamic vinegar and mustard in a bowl. Add the chicken and let it marinade for 30 minutes. Discard the marinade.
2. In the meantime, press the STEAM button on your Hamilton Beach Rice Cooker and set timer to 80 minutes.
3. Add the oil and heat it.
4. Stir in the shallots and cook for 5 minutes.
5. Add the mushrooms and cook for 6-8 minutes. Then, stir in the farro and cook for another 3-5 minutes.
6. Finally, discard the marinade and place the chicken inside the cooker.
7. Close the lid and cook for 1 hour.
8. Once it goes off, the pot will switch to WARM mode.
9. Carefully open the lid, sprinkle with freshly chopped parsley and serve immediately.

Nutrition Info: Calories: 421 Fat: 7g Carbohydrates: 60g Protein: 30

28. Beef And Cabbage Roll

Servings: 2
Cooking Time: 15 Minutes
Ingredients:

- 10 Napa cabbage leaves, blanched
- ½ pound beef tenderloins, thinly sliced
- 3 ounces white mushrooms
- Salt and pepper to taste

Directions:

1. Place the Napa leaves on a flat surface. Arrange the beef slices on top the leaves, and season with salt and pepper. Top with sliced mushrooms.

2. Roll in the cabbage and enclose the beef inside. Place on a plate that can fit in your steaming basket.
3. Place the steaming basket in your Hamilton Beach Cooker. Add water up to line
4. Close the lid, push STEAM, and set timer to 15 minutes. Let the cook cycle complete, then carefully open the lid and serve warm.

Nutrition Info: Calories: 546 Fat: 30g Carbohydrates: 43g Protein: 26g

29. Meatballs From Sweden

Servings: 4
Cooking Time: 30 Minutes
Ingredients:

- 1 pound ground beef
- 4 cups breadcrumbs
- 2 tablespoons mustard
- 1 whole egg
- 2 teaspoons beef bouillon granules
- 2 cups heavy cream
- 1 white onion, chopped
- Salt and pepper to taste
- 2 tablespoons of oil

Directions:

1. Take a bowl and add ground beef, bread crumbs, salt, egg and pepper.
2. Mix well and form 2-inch meatballs. Push the STEAM button and set the timer to 30 minutes. Heat the oil and cook the meatballs until browned, about 7-10 minutes.
3. Remove the seared meatballs from your cooker and set aside.
4. Next, add the mustard, heavy cream, beef bouillon granules to your cooker.
5. Stir well and return the meatballs. Close the lid, press STEAM mode and let the cycle complete.
6. Once it goes off, carefully open the lid and serve immediately.

Nutrition Info: Calories: 377 Fat: 29g Carbohydrates: 11g Protein: 17g

30. Beautiful Curried Squash And Pork

Servings: 4
Cooking Time: 60 Minutes
Ingredients:

- 1 tablespoon peanut oil
- 1 lb boneless sirloin pork chop, diced
- 1 ½ tablespoon curry powder
- 2 carrots, sliced
- ½ onion, chopped
- 1 teaspoon fresh garlic, minced
- 14 ounce can chicken broth, undiluted
- 13 ounce low –fat coconut milk
- ¼ cup water
- 1 19 ounce can chickpeas, drained and rinsed
- ¾ cup uncooked brown rice
- 1 cup raw acorn squash, diced

Directions:

1. Push the STEAM button and set timer to 15 minutes.
2. Add the oil heat it. Then add the meat and close the lid.
3. Make sure to open the lid every 5 minutes to turn the meat.
4. Next, add the vegetables and cook for 5 minutes more.
5. Cancel the STEAM function and add all the remaining ingredients.
6. Give it a good stir and close the lid.
7. Push BROWN RICE and let cooking cycle complete.
8. Once it goes off, the cooker will switch to WARM mode.
9. Carefully open the lid and serve immediately.

Nutrition Info: Calories: 256 Fat: 9g Carbohydrates: 19g Protein: 26g

31. Delicious Whole Chicken

Servings: 4-6

Cooking Time: 40-50 Minutes
Ingredients:

- A 3-pound chicken
- 2 small onions, peeled, cut in half
- 1 lemon, cut in half
- 2 sprigs rosemary
- 2 tablespoon butter
- Salt and pepper to taste

Directions:

1. Place the onions flat on the bottom of your Hamilton Beach cooker.
2. Stuff the lemon halves in the chicken along with the rosemary.
3. Coat chicken generously with butter and season with salt and pepper.
4. Place chicken in your rice cooker on top of the sliced onions.
5. Close the lid, press WHITE RICE, and let the cooking cycle complete.
6. Once it goes off, carefully open the lid.
7. Turn around the chicken and push WHITE RICE again, close the lid and let another cooking cycle to complete.
8. Once ready, take the chicken out and broil under a broiler for about 5 minutes for a crispy finish (only if the chicken is slightly undercooked).
9. Serve immediately and enjoy.

Nutrition Info: Calories: 399 Fat: 27g Carbohydrates: 13g Protein: 34g

SOUPS, STEWS AND CHILIES

32. A Fine Taco Soup

Servings: 6
Cooking Time: 50 Minutes
Ingredients:

- 5 cups chicken stock
- 1 small white onion, diced
- 1 cup corn kernels
- 2 carrots, diced small
- 3 chicken breasts, skinless and boneless, diced
- 1 12 ounce can diced tomatoes
- 1 garlic clove, minced
- ½ cup black beans, rinsed
- ½ cup brown rice
- 1 tablespoon olive oil
- Salt to taste

Directions:

1. Push STEAM button and set the timer to 10 minutes.
2. Pour the oil and heat it.
3. Add onion and garlic and cook for 2 minutes, or until the onion is translucent.
4. Add the chicken and cook for 5 minutes until brown.
5. Then add the chicken stock, tomatoes, rice, carrots, corn and beans.
6. Close the lid and press the BROWN RICE button, allowing the cooking cycle to complete.
7. Once it goes off, open the lid and serve hot.
8. Serve and enjoy!

Nutrition Info: Calories: 149 Fat: 4g Carbohydrates: 18g Protein: 12g

33. Authentic Tortellini Soup

Servings: 6
Cooking Time: 20 Minutes

Ingredients:

- 2 tablespoons butter
- 1 white onion, diced
- 4 cloves garlic, minced
- 2 tablespoons roasted red pepper, diced
- 4 cups chicken broth
- 1 28 ounce can diced tomatoes, with juice
- 1 15-oz can pinto beans, drained and rinsed
- 1 cup heavy cream
- ⅓ cup parmesan cheese, grated
- 2 tablespoons Italian seasoning
- Salt and pepper, to taste
- 12 ounces refrigerated tortellini
- 4 large handfuls spinach

Directions:

1. Push the STEAM button and set timer to 5 minutes.
2. Once hot, add butter and melt.
3. Stir in onion, garlic, roasted pepper and cook for 2 minutes, until soft and translucent.
4. Add broth, pinto beans, tomatoes, heavy cream, seasoning and cheese.
5. Close the lid and bring it to a simmer. Carefully open the lid and add spinach and tortellini.
6. Let simmer for 10 minutes until the soup thickens.
7. Top with freshly grated parmesan cheese and serve.

Nutrition Info: Calories: 487 Fat: 26g Carbohydrates: 65g Protein: 34g

34. Fascinating Rice Chili Stew

Servings: 6
Cooking Time: 25 Minutes
Ingredients:

- ½ cup white rice

- ¼ cup cooked black beans
- ¼ cup sweet corn
- 1 garlic clove, minced
- 1 teaspoon ginger paste
- 1 teaspoon cumin powder
- 1 teaspoon chili pepper
- 1 teaspoon oregano
- 1 avocado, sliced
- 1 teaspoon lemon juice
- 1 ½ cups water

Directions:

1. Add all the listed ingredients to your Hamilton Beach cooker except for the avocado and lemon juice.
2. Close the lid, press the STEAM button, and set timer to 25 minutes.
3. Once the cycle is complete, carefully open the lid and drizzle lemon juice.
4. Serve topped with sliced avocados and enjoy!

Nutrition Info: Calories: 306 Fat: 9g Carbohydrates: 45g Protein: 14g

35. A Fine Vegetable Stew

Servings: 4
Cooking Time: 25 Minutes
Ingredients:

- 1 Napa cabbage, cut into 2 inch slices
- 1 ½ cups warm water
- 1 teaspoon oyster sauce
- 3 ounces mung bean, soaked in water for 5 minutes
- 2 teaspoons brown sugar
- 1 tablespoon salted soybeans, mashed
- 8 ounces white mushrooms, sliced
- 10 ounces tofu, cut into slices
- Salt and pepper to taste

Directions:

1. In a mid size bowl, add sugar, oyster sauce, ½ of cup water, and mix well.
2. Press the STEAM button and set the timer to 25 minutes.
3. Add oil to the rice cooker and heat it.
4. Add the mashed soy beans and cook for 3 minutes.
5. Then add the rest the ingredients and close the lid. Cook for 17-20 minutes.
6. Once the cooking is over, carefully open the lid and adjust the seasoning.
7. Serve hot.

Nutrition Info: Calories: 468 Fat: 21g Carbohydrates: 66g Protein: 19g

36. Tantalizing Split Pea Soup

Servings: 4
Cooking Time: 60 Minutes
Ingredients:

- 1 cup yellow split peas
- 4 cups vegetable broth
- ½ bay leaf
- ¼ teaspoon ground coriander seeds
- ½ tablespoon olive oil
- Salt and pepper to taste

Directions:

1. Add all ingredients to your Hamilton Beach rice cooker and gently stir.
2. Close the lid, push the STEAM button, and set timer to 60 minutes.
3. Once the cooking cycle is over, carefully open the lid and season to taste.
4. Serve and enjoy!

Nutrition Info: Calories: 360 Fat: 12g Carbohydrates: 49g Protein: 16g

37. Pork And Mushroom Creamy Stew

Servings: 4
Cooking Time: 30 Minutes
Ingredients:

- For Grains
- 4 tablespoons water
- 4 large asparagus spears, tough ends removed sliced into 1-inch long slivers
- 1 cup white rice, rinsed and drained
- Dash sea salt
- For Stew
- 1 pound pork tenderloin, trimmed with membranes remove and sliced into ¼ inch thick half-moons, rinsed and patted dry using kitchen towel
- ¼ pound baby carrots, tops remove and skin scrubbed clean, unpeeled
- 1 can 15-oz whole button mushrooms, small caps, rinsed and drained
- 1 can 15-oz straw mushrooms, rinsed and drained whole
- 1 small red bell pepper, deseeded and ribbed, cubed
- 1 cup sour cream
- 1 cup mushroom broth
- 1 teaspoon fish sauce
- Salt and pepper to taste
- Water
- 1 tablespoon fresh parsley, minced for garnish

Directions:

1. Take a large sheet of aluminum foil and make a pouch with sealed edges.
2. Place all the rice ingredients in the pouch and stir. Seal the edges and set the pouch in a steamer tray.
3. Add all the listed stew ingredients to your Hamilton Beach Pot except the sour cream, water and parsley. Pour water to line Place steamer tray in your Rice Cooker.

4. Close the lid and push STEAM button, set timer to 25 minutes.
5. One the cooking cycle completes, turn the cooker off and remove steam steamer tray. Let the pouch cool. Stir well the stew and adjust seasoning.
6. Serve by spooning the stew mix and topping with a portion the rice and peas mix. Garnish with parsley if needed.

Nutrition Info: Calories: 462 Fat: 28g Carbohydrates: 14g Protein: 37g

38. Healthy Veggie Lentil Soup

Servings: 8
Cooking Time: 50 Minutes
Ingredients:

- 8 ounces fire roasted tomatoes
- 2 carrots, diced
- 6 cups vegetable broth
- ¼ teaspoon ground coriander seeds
- 1 tablespoon olive oil
- 8 ounces brown lentils, rinsed
- 2 celery stalks, chopped
- ¼ teaspoon ground cumin
- Salt and pepper to taste

Directions:

1. Add the listed ingredients to your Hamilton Beach Cooker. Give it a good stir.
2. Push STEAM button and set timer to 50 minutes. Allow the mixture to reach simmer, with the lid open. Then close the lid and let the STEAM cycle to complete. Once done, carefully Open the lid and season to taste.

Nutrition Info: Calories: 268 Fat: 1g Carbohydrates: 50g Protein: 17g

39. Spicy Lemongrass Shrimp Bowl

Servings: 4
Cooking Time: 25 Minutes
Ingredients:

- 1 pound uncooked jumbo shrimp, peeled and deveined
- 2 carrots, sliced diagonally
- 2 celery stalks, sliced diagonally
- ½ onion, sliced diagonally
- 2 cloves garlic, thinly sliced
- 2 large slices fresh ginger
- 2 tablespoons red pepper flakes
- 1 lemongrass stalk
- 4 cups vegetable broth
- 2 tablespoons coconut oil

Directions:

1. Prepare the lemongrass by removing the tough outer leaves and cutting the stalk into 2-3 inch pieces.
2. Bruise the stalk by bending them several time.
3. Push the STEAM button and set timer to 25 minutes.
4. Add in the oil heat it.
5. Then add in the vegetables, ginger, garlic and sauté for 10 minutes, stirring occasionally.
6. Add broth and red pepper flakes, close the lid and cook for 10 minutes.
7. After that, open the lid and add the shrimp.
8. Keep cooking for 2-3 more minutes until the shrimp are barely pink.
9. Serve warm.

Nutrition Info: Calories: 115 Fat: 1g Carbohydrates: 9g Protein: 17g

40. Lentils Kale Miso Soup

Servings: 6
Cooking Time: 20 Minutes
Ingredients:

- ½ cup lentils
- 7-8 kale leaves, chopped
- ¼ cup sweet corn
- 1 tablespoon Miso paste
- 1 teaspoon sea salt
- 1 garlic clove, minced
- ½ teaspoon pepper powder
- 1 cup water

Directions:

1. Add all the listed ingredients to your Hamilton Beach cooker.
2. Push the STEAM button and set timer to 20 minutes.
3. Close the lid and let the cooking cycle complete.
4. Once done, carefully open the lid and stir. Serve the soup hot and enjoy!

Nutrition Info: Calories: 256 Fat: 8g Carbohydrates: 45g Protein: 8g

41. Coolest Rice Beef Soup

Servings: 6
Cooking Time: 1 Hour 30 Minutes
Ingredients:

- 1 ½ cups long-grain rice
- 10 cups water
- 1 tablespoon fresh parsley, chopped
- 1 tablespoon fresh chives, chopped
- 1 tablespoon fresh rosemary, chopped
- Salt and pepper to taste
- ½ teaspoon cinnamon, ground
- 2 pounds beef, cubed

Directions:

1. Add rice, parsley, water, chives, rosemary and pepper to your Hamilton Beach cooker.

2. Close the lid and press WHITE RICE, and cook on the preset amount of time.
3. Once ready, the cooker will switch to WARM mode.
4. Open the lid and add the beef and cinnamon.
5. Stir well and close the lid.
6. Press WHITE RICE again and allow the cooking cycle to complete.
7. Carefully open the lid and serve warm.

Nutrition Info: Calories: 230 Fat: 7g Carbohydrates: 25g Protein: 17g

42. Chicken White Radish Soup

Servings: 3
Cooking Time: 90 Minutes
Ingredients:

- ½ pound chicken breasts, skinless and chopped
- 5 ginger slices
- 1 white radish (daikon), peeled and cut to large chunks
- 8 shiitake mushrooms, stem removed
- 1 tablespoon wolfberries, soaked until puffy, drained
- 3 dried scallops
- Salt and pepper to taste
- 5 cups water

Directions:

1. Add 2 cups water and fill up to line 2.
2. Press STEAM and set timer to 20 minutes.
3. Once the water starts to boil, add chicken and cook for 8-10 minutes, with the lid closed.
4. Then, discard the water and keep the chicken inside.
5. Add 3 cups of water and cover the chicken pieces.
6. Once the water starts to boil again, add daikon, mushrooms, dried scallops and ginger.
7. Close the lid and press WHITE RICE, let the cycle complete.
8. Once the cooker switches to WARM, let it sit for 1.5-2 hours in WARM mode.

9. About 30 minutes prior to serving, add the soaked wolfberries.
10. Season and enjoy!

Nutrition Info: Calories: 345 Fat: 19g Carbohydrates: 38g Protein: 8g

43. Extra Creamy Mushroom Soup

Servings: 4
Cooking Time: 25 Minutes
Ingredients:

- 1 cup button mushrooms, diced
- 1 white onion, sliced
- 2 garlic cloves, minced
- ¼ cup coconut milk
- ½ cup water
- Sea salt and pepper to taste
- 1 teaspoon coconut oil

Directions:

1. Push STEAM button and set timer to 25 minutes. Add oil and heat it.
2. Then add the garlic, onion and mushrooms and sauté for 2 minutes. Add the rest of the ingredients, except for the coconut milk. Close the lid and cook on STEAM mode for 20 minutes.
3. Once the cooking cycle is complete, open the lid and let the soup cool.
4. Stir in coconut milk and blend the soup using an immersion blender.

Nutrition Info: Calories: 368 Fat: 9g Carbohydrates: 63g Protein: 10g

44. Grand Ma's Chicken Soup

Servings: 4
Cooking Time: 20 Minutes
Ingredients:

- 2 boneless and skinless chicken breast, diced
- 4 cups chicken stock

- 1 yellow onion, diced
- 2 garlic cloves, minced
- 1 cup baby spinach
- 1 carrot, cut into thin rounds
- ½ cup frozen broccoli
- ½ cup frozen cauliflower
- 2 cups egg noodle
- ½ tablespoon olive oil
- Salt to taste

Directions:

1. Push the STEAM button and set timer to 20 minutes. Add oil and heat it. Add in onion, garlic, carrots and cook for 2 minutes.
2. Then add the chicken and vegetables and sauté for 6-7 minutes. Next, add the chicken stock and season. Allow the mixture to reach a boil and add the noodles.
3. Cook until the noodles are tender and spinach have wilted. Serve warm.

Nutrition Info: Calories: 229 Fat: 13g Carbohydrates: 11g Protein: 18g

45. Very Comforting Beef Stew

Servings: 4
Cooking Time: 45 Minutes
Ingredients:

- 1 pound beef stew meat
- ½ large potato, diced
- ½ cup peas
- ½ medium carrot, diced
- 12 ounces tomato puree
- 1 cup celery, diced
- ½ cup butter bean
- 2 tablespoons vegetable oil
- ½ cup water
- 1 teaspoon garlic, minced

- 2 tablespoons dry onion soup mix
- ¼ cup capsicum, diced

Directions:

1. Push the STEAM button and set timer to 10 minutes. Pour oil and heat it. Add the beef and cook for 5 minutes until brown.
2. Add the rest of the ingredients and stir well. Seal the lid, press the BROWN RICE button, and let the cooking cycle to complete. Carefully open the lid and serve hot.

Nutrition Info: Calories: 468 Fat: 23g Carbohydrates: 17g Protein: 46g

46. Exquisite Clam Chowder

Servings: 4-6
Cooking Time: 30 Minutes
Ingredients:

- 2 tablespoons butter
- 1 cup onion, chopped
- 1 cup celery leaves, chopped
- 2 garlic cloves, chopped
- 2 cups fingerling potatoes, cubed
- 1 tablespoon flour
- 2 cups vegetable stock
- 1 cup heavy cream
- 1 can 16 ounce clams, chopped
- 1 bay leaf
- 1 sprig fresh thyme

Directions:

1. Push the STEAM button and set timer to 20 minutes.
2. Add butter and melt it.
3. Stir in the onion, garlic and celery and cook for 2-3 minutes.
4. Mix in the flour, and then pour the vegetable stock, bay leaf, sprig thyme and potatoes.

5. Close the lid and let the cycle complete.
6. Open the lid and stir in the cream and chopped clams with juice.
7. Close the lid again and cook for 5 minutes more. Serve warm and enjoy.

Nutrition Info: Calories: 436 Fat: 20g Carbohydrates: 39g Protein: 27g

47. Pork And Vegetable Spicy Stew

Servings: 4
Cooking Time: 50 Minutes
Ingredients:

- For Rice
- 4 tablespoon water
- 1 cup white rice, rinsed and drained
- For Stew
- 1 pound pork belly, sliced into inch thick cubes
- ¼ pound winged beans, ends removed sliced into inch long slivers
- 2 pieces large, red ripe tomatoes, quartered
- 1 piece, large daikon white radish, peeled and sliced into ¼ inch medallions
- 1 piece medium shallot, peeled and quarter
- 1 small taro, peeled and sliced into inch thick cubes
- 1 tablespoon tamarind paste
- 1 teaspoon fish sauce
- ½ teaspoon black peppercorns
- Kosher salt as needed
- Water as needed

Directions:

1. Take a large sheet of aluminum foil and make a pouch with sealed edges.
2. Pour in water and rice and seal edges.
3. Transfer to a steamer tray.
4. Add the stew ingredients to the Hamilton Beach Cooker, except for the water.

5. Add water to line 4. Place the steamer tray on top.
6. Close the lid and push the STEAM button and set timer to 45 minutes.
7. Once the cooking cycle is complete, carefully open the lid and remove the pouch.
8. Let it cool.
9. Stir the stew and adjust the seasoning.
10. Serve by taking the rice from the pouch and dividing it into serving bowls.
11. Ladle 1 portion of the stew on top.

Nutrition Info: Calories: 224 Fat: 10g Carbohydrates: 25g Protein: 10g

RICE AND OTHER GRAINS

48. Authentic Thai Chicken Rice

Servings: 4
Cooking Time: 35-45 Minutes
Ingredients:

- 1 red pepper, sliced
- 3 cups rice, washed and uncooked
- 2 chicken breasts, cubed
- For Sauce
- 1 can chunked pineapple with ¼ cup juice
- 1 can milk, coconut
- ½ teaspoon ginger, powdered
- 1 tablespoon ginger, grated
- 1 teaspoon five spice powder, Chinese

Directions:

1. Add the rice to your Hamilton Beach cooker and pour water up to line 3.
2. Close the lid, push the WHITE RICE button, and let the cooking cycle complete.
3. In the meantime, heat 1 tablespoon of oil in a small pan over medium heat.
4. Add in the chicken cubes and cook them for 4-5 minutes or until slightly undercooked.
5. Once the chicken is almost cooked, lower down the heat to low.
6. Take a bowl and whisk in all the sauce ingredients.
7. Pour the sauce over the chicken and cook for 8-10 minutes.
8. Once the Hamilton Beach cooker completes the cycle and switches to WARM mode, transfer the rice to a serving platter.
9. Serve a portion the rice with the sauce and the chicken on top.

Nutrition Info: Calories: 489 Fat: 32g Carbohydrates: 79g Protein: 36g

49. Spicy Cajun Crawfish Tails With Rice

Servings: 4
Cooking Time: 45 Minutes
Ingredients:

- 1 ½ cups uncooked long-grain rice
- 1 green bell pepper, diced
- 1 small onion, diced
- 1 bunch green onions, diced
- 1 pound peeled crawfish tails
- 1 (14 ounce) can chicken broth
- 1 (10 ounce) can diced tomatoes with green chile pepper
- 4 tablespoons butter
- 1 tablespoon dried parsley
- 1 teaspoon Cajun seasoning

Directions:

1. Add rice, onion, green pepper, green onion, crawfish tails, chicken broth, diced tomatoes, parsley, butter, Cajun seasoning in a large bowl.
2. Mix well and pour the mixture into your Hamilton Beach Cooker.
3. Close the lid, push the WHITE RICE button, and let the cooking cycle complete. When ready, open the lid and season to taste before serving.

Nutrition Info: Calories: 462 Fat: 27g Carbohydrates: 55g Protein: 22g

50. "pirates Of The Caribbean" Rice

Servings: 4
Cooking Time: 30-40 Minutes
Ingredients:

- 1 cup white rice, rinsed
- 1 teaspoon ground Jamaican jerk spiced
- 1 sprig thyme, stem discarded
- 1 garlic clove, minced
- 1 teaspoon ginger, grated
- 2 scallions, sliced

- ¾ cup sweet potatoes, finely diced
- ⅓ cup toasted coconut flakes
- ⅓ cup raisins
- ⅓ cup red pepper, diced
- 1 cup vegetable broth

Directions:

1. Add all the listed ingredients to your Hamilton Beach Cooker, except for the scallions and coconut flakes.
2. Pour broth and close the lid. Press WHITE RICE and let the cooking cycle complete. When ready, carefully open the lid and fluff the rice with a fork.
3. Transfer to a serving dish and garnish with coconut and scallions.

Nutrition Info: Calories: 278 Fat: 24g Carbohydrates: 15g Protein: 4g

51. Very "wild" Rice

Servings: 8
Cooking Time: 65-75 Minutes
Ingredients:

- 2 cups wild rice, rinsed and drained
- 4 cups unsalted chicken stock
- Butter for grease
- Salt to taste

Directions:

1. Grease the inner cooking pot with butter. Add the rice and season with salt.
2. Fill the cooker with water up to line 2 mark. Stir and close the lid.
3. Push the BROWN RICE button and let the cooking cycle complete.
4. Once the Hamilton Beach Pot switches to WARM mode, let the rice simmer for 10 minutes. After that, fluff the rice and transfer to serving bowls.

Nutrition Info: Calories: 200 Fat: 2g Carbohydrates: 36g Protein: 10g

52. Beautiful Lemon Rice

Servings: 4
Cooking Time: 30-40 Minutes
Ingredients:

- 1 cup long-grain white rice
- 1 ½ cups vegetable stock
- 1 pinch salt
- 1 large garlic clove
- Zest of ½ lemon, freshly grated
- 2 tablespoons unsalted butter
- 2 tablespoons fresh Italian parsley

Directions:

1. Add the rice, stock and salt to your Hamilton Beach cooker. Stir and top with garlic.
2. Close the lid, select WHITE RICE and let the cooking cycle complete.
3. When ready, the cooker will switch to WARM mode. Press STEAM and let the rice cook for 10 minutes more. Fluff with a spoon, discard garlic and serve hot!

Nutrition Info: Calories: 391 Fat: 4g Carbohydrates: 69g Protein: 8g

53. Amazing Ginger And Chicken Rice

Servings: 4
Cooking Time: 45 Minutes
Ingredients:

- 1 large chicken bouillon cube
- ¾ cup hot water
- 1 cup jasmine rice
- 1 ¼ pounds skinless, boneless chicken thighs cut into 1-inch cubes

- 1 2-inch piece of fresh ginger, peeled and cut into matchsticks
- 3 packed cups baby spinach
- 1 cup unsweetened coconut milk
- Salt to taste

Directions:

1. Take a small bowl with hot water and dissolve bouillon cube.
2. Add rice, chicken and ginger to your Hamilton Beach Cooker.
3. Arrange spinach on top and pour in the coconut milk and bouillon broth. Salt to taste.
4. Close the lid, push the WHITE RICE button, and let the cooking cycle complete.
5. Once the cooker switches to WARM mode, let it sit for 5 minutes with the lid closed. Open the lid and fluff the rice with a fork before serving.

Nutrition Info: Calories: 467 Fat: 29g Carbohydrates: 11g Protein: 38g

54. Traditional Basmati Rice

Servings: 6
Cooking Time: 30-35 Minutes
Ingredients:

- 2 cups Basmati rice, rinsed and drained
- Water, to fill up to line 2
- Salt to taste
- Fresh parsley, chopped

Directions:

1. Add the rice to your Hamilton Beach Cooker. Fill inner pot with water up to line 2.
2. Stir and close the lid. Press WHITE RICE and let the cooking cycle complete.
3. Once the cooker switches to WARM mode, open the lid and allow it to sit for 10 min. Fluff the rice and garnish with parsley before serving.

Nutrition Info: Calories: 234 Fat: 0g Carbohydrates: 47g Protein: 4g

55. Creamy Chicken Mushroom Rice

Servings: 4
Cooking Time: 45-55 Minutes
Ingredients:

- 2 chicken breasts, halved and julienned
- 4 cups uncooked white rice, rinsed well
- 2 cups chicken broth
- ½ cup dried shiitake mushrooms
- ½ cup frozen peas, unthawed
- ½ cup table cream
- 1 teaspoon fish sauce
- Dash black pepper
- Dash kosher salt
- Water
- ¼ cup fresh cilantro, minced for garnish

Directions:

1. Add dried mushrooms in a bowl and soak them in 2 cups of water for 1 hour.
2. Remove and discard the stem. Mince the cap. Reserve 1 cup of the soaking liquid.
3. Lay the chicken fillets in steamer tray and season with salt and pepper.
4. Place all the ingredients to your Hamilton Beach Cooker except for the chicken and cream.
5. Add water to 4 level mark. Place steam tray on top.
6. Close the lid, push the WHITE RICE button, and let the cooking cycle complete.
7. When done, remove the lid and take the steamer tray out.
8. Fold in cream into the rice and stir. Add the steamed chicken to the rice and stir.
9. Sprinkle with freshly minced cilantro and serve immediately.

Nutrition Info: Calories: 165 Fat: 4g Carbohydrates: 15g Protein: 16g

56. Hearty Bacon Rice

Servings: 4
Cooking Time: 30 Minutes
Ingredients:

- 2 cups white rice
- 2 cups beef stock
- 1 tablespoon oil
- 8 ounces bacon, cut in strips
- 1 onion, sliced
- 1 teaspoon garlic, minced
- 1 cup frozen mixed vegetables
- 2 tablespoons soy sauce

Directions:

1. Push the STEAM button and set timer to 10 minutes.
2. Heat oil and stir in the bacon and onion.
3. Sauté for 4-5 minutes or until the onion is translucent.
4. Add in the garlic and cook for another minute.
5. Next, add the rice and stir to coat well.
6. Add the vegetables, beef stock and stir gently.
7. Close the lid, push the WHITE RICE button, and let the cooking cycle complete.
8. When ready, carefully open the lid and stir in soy sauce.
9. Serve immediately and enjoy.

Nutrition Info: Calories: 525 Fat: 28g Carbohydrates: 70g Protein: 29g

57. Authentic Spanish Rice

Servings: 8
Cooking Time: 35 Minutes
Ingredients:

- 2 cups long-grain white rice
- 2 cups water
- 1 (8 ounce) can tomato sauce
- 14 ounces Mexican Style stewed tomatoes, with juice
- ¼ cup salsa
- ¾ teaspoon cumin
- ¾ teaspoon garlic salt
- 2 teaspoons chili powder
- 1 ½ teaspoons dried onion
- ¾ teaspoon salt
- 1 small green pepper, diced
- 1 can diced green chilies, optional

Directions:

1. Grease the inner pot of your Hamilton Beach cooker with cooking spray.
2. Add the rice and 2 cups of water along with the other ingredients and stir well.
3. Close the lid, push the WHITE RICE button, and near the end of the cooking cycle check if the rice is cooked properly. If not, cook it until the desired consistency.
4. Once the Hamilton Beach Cooker switches to WARM mode, let it sit for 5 minutes.
5. Carefully open the lid and serve.

Nutrition Info: Calories: 328 Fat: 6g Carbohydrates: 58g Protein: 8g

58. Chicken And Ginger Rice Meal

Servings: 4
Cooking Time: 20-30 Minutes
Ingredients:

- 1 cup coconut milk, unsweetened
- 3 cups baby spinach, packed
- 1 piece 2-inch long sliced ginger, peeled
- 1 ¼ pounds chicken breasts, cubed and boneless

- 1 cup jasmine rice, washed
- ¾ cup water
- 1 large bouillon cube, chicken
- Salt to taste

Directions:

1. Take a bowl full of hot water and dissolve bouillon cube.
2. Add chicken, ginger and rice to your Hamilton Beach Cooker.
3. Arrange spinach on top.
4. Pour broth and coconut milk and give it a good stir.
5. Season with salt and close the lid.
6. Push the WHITE RICE button and wait for the cooking cycle to complete.
7. When ready, the cooker will switch to WARM mode. Let the mixture stand for 5 minutes. Open the lid, and fluff the rice.
8. Serve immediately.

Nutrition Info: Calories: 296 Fat: 6g Carbohydrates: 24g Protein: 34g

59. Sesame Chicken Rice

Servings: 6
Cooking Time: 35 Minutes
Ingredients:

- 2 tablespoons peanut oil
- 1 teaspoon sesame oil
- 1 tablespoon finely grated fresh ginger
- 2 garlic cloves, peeled and crushed
- 2 onions, peeled and sliced
- 2 cups short grain rice
- 2 cups cooked chicken, chopped
- ¼ cup shallots, chopped
- 2 tablespoons sesame seeds, toasted
- 3 cups chicken stock

Directions:

1. Set your Hamilton Beach Cooker to STEAM mode and set timer to 5 minutes.
2. Heat the oils, and add in ginger, onions and garlic. Stir-fry for 2 minutes.
3. Add the washed rice, stir and cook for another minute.
4. Pour chicken stock and close the lid. Press WHITE RICE and let the cycle complete. Once it goes off, open the lid and mix in chicken, sesame seeds and shallots.
5. Close the lid and let it simmer in WARM mode for 10 minutes before serving.

Nutrition Info: Calories 422 Fat: 27g Carbohydrates: 62g Protein: 32g

60. Rocking And Flying Risotto

Servings: 4
Cooking Time: 40-45 Minutes
Ingredients:

- 2 tablespoons olive oil
- 16 ounces mushrooms, sliced
- 3 tablespoons butter
- 2 cups Arborio rice
- 1 shallot, diced
- 1 clove garlic, minced
- ½ cup white wine
- 4 ½ cups chicken broth
- 1 teaspoon salt
- ½ teaspoon black pepper
- ⅓ cup grated parmesan
- ⅔ cup peas
- 1 tablespoon butter

Directions:

1. Heat oil in a skillet over medium heat. Add the mushrooms and shallots and cook for 5-7 minutes or until tender. Then, remove from heat and set aside.

2. Push the STEAM button of your Hamilton Beach Rice Cooker and set the timer to 35 minutes.
3. Melt butter and add in the rice. Stir in garlic, wine, 2 cups of stock, salt and pepper.
4. Close the lid and cook for 10 minutes.
5. Once ready, open the lid and stir in the mushrooms and rest of the stock.
6. Cook for 17 more minutes. Stir in peas and 1 tablespoon of butter.
7. Sprinkle with freshly grated parmesan cheese and serve immediately.

Nutrition Info: Calories 247 Fat: 7g Carbohydrates: 32g Protein: 12g

61. Delicious Saffron Yellow Rice With Fruit Chutney

Servings: 6
Cooking Time: 35 Minutes
Ingredients:

- 3 cups basmati rice, rinsed
- 3 cups water
- 1 pinch powdered saffron
- 2 tablespoons fruit chutney
- 2-4 cardamom pods, split and use seeds
- Salt and Pepper, to taste
- 1 ounce butter
- 2-4 sprigs fresh coriander, optional

Directions:

1. Place 3 cups Basmati rice in your Hamilton Beach Cooker. Pour water up to line 3.
2. Add saffron, cardamom seeds, chutney. Season with salt and pepper.
3. Close the lid, push the WHITE RICE button, and let the cooking cycle complete.
4. Once it goes off, carefully open the lid and stir in butter, mix gently to combine. Garnish with freshly chopped coriander and top with toasted flakes.

Nutrition Info: Calories: 314 Fat: 2g Carbohydrates: 76g Protein: 3g

62. Brown Rice Tabbouleh

Servings: 4
Cooking Time: 35 -40 Minutes
Ingredients:

- 1 ½ cups medium-grain brown rice
- 2 cups water
- ½ a teaspoon salt
- 2 small tomatoes, ripe, cut into small cubes
- 1 ½ cup European cucumber, cut into small cubes
- 1 ½ cup green onion, minced
- ⅛ cup mint leaves, chopped
- ⅛ cup extra virgin olive oil
- 1 tablespoon lemon juice
- 1 pinch paprika
- Salt and pepper to taste

Directions:

1. Rinse the rice under cold water and drain, then transfer to your Hamilton Beach Cooker.
2. Add water and season with salt.
3. Give it a gentle stir and close the lid.
4. Press BROWN RICE and let the cooking cycle complete.
5. When ready, open the lid and fluff the rice with a fork.
6. Transfer the rice to a large plate and let it sit for 30 minutes.
7. Take another bowl and mix in the remaining ingredients.
8. Season with salt and pepper.
9. Once the rice is cool, add the previously prepared mixture to the rice and toss well to mix everything up.
10. Serve and enjoy!

Nutrition Info: Calories: 267 Fat: 12g Carbohydrates: 37g Protein: 5g

63. Peanut Butter Rice

Servings: 4
Cooking Time: 20-30 Minutes
Ingredients:

- 3 bell peppers, finely chopped
- 1 cup soaked white rice
- ¼ cup peanut butter
- ¼ cup tomato puree
- 1 teaspoon paprika powder
- 1 teaspoon salt
- 2 cups water

Directions:

1. In a bowl, mix in water and peanut butter, then set aside for 10 minutes.
2. Add the rest of the ingredients to your Hamilton Beach Cooker. Give it a good stir and add in the peanut butter mix.
3. Close the lid, push the WHITE RICE button, and let the cooking cycle complete. When done, carefully open the lid, stir and serve warm.

Nutrition Info: Calories: 107 Fat: 8g Carbohydrates: 6g Protein: 1g

64. Berryful Goldilocks Porridge

Servings: 4
Cooking Time: 10 Minutes
Ingredients:

- 1 cup brown rice farina
- 1 cup low-fat milk
- ½ cup strawberries, sliced
- ¼ cup sour cream
- 2 tablespoons honey
- 2 cups water
- 1 pinch brown sugar

Directions:

1. Add farina to the rice cooker. Stir in milk and 2 cups of water.
2. Close the lid, press the STEAM button, and cook for 10 minutes.
3. Open the lid after 5 minutes and give it a good stir.
4. Once cooking is complete, carefully open the rice cooker's lid, keeping hands and face away to avoid steam burns.
5. Divide the porridge between 4 bowls.
6. Top with strawberries, sour cream and honey.
7. Drizzle with brown sugar and serve.

Nutrition Info: Calories: 385 Fat 12g Carbohydrates: 48g Protein: 7g

65. Cashew And Cherry Rice

Servings: 4
Cooking Time: 20-30 Minutes
Ingredients:

- ½ cup long-grain white rice
- ½ cup fresh cherries, chopped
- ¼ cup cashew paste
- ½ teaspoon salt
- ¼ teaspoon cinnamon powder
- ½ cup almond milk
- ½ cup water

Directions:

1. Add all of the ingredients to your Hamilton Beach Cooker. Stir gently.
2. Close the lid, push the WHITE RICE button, and let the cooking cycle complete.
3. Once the cooker switches to WARM mode, let it simmer for 7-10 minutes.
4. Open the lid, stir and serve warm.

Nutrition Info: Calories: 453 Fat: 26g Carbohydrates: 88g Protein: 21g

66. Healthy Mexican Green Rice

Servings: 4
Cooking Time: 30 Minutes
Ingredients:

- 1 tablespoon unsalted butter
- ½ small white onion, chopped
- 1 cup long-grain white rice
- 1 ½ cups water
- ½ teaspoon salt
- ½ cup fresh cilantro leaves, minced

Directions:

1. Push the STEAM button and set timer to 5 minutes.
2. Melt the butter and stir in the onions. Sauté for 2-3 minutes until translucent.
3. Add in rice, salt, water, cilantro and give it a good stir.
4. Close the lid, push the BROWN RICE button, and let the cooking cycle complete.
5. Once the cooker switches to WARM mode, press the STEAM button and let the rice STEAM for 15 minutes.
6. Once ready, fluff the rice and serve.

Nutrition Info: Calories: 129 Fat: 7g Carbohydrates: 13g Protein: 5g

67. Jasmine Rice Pilaf

Servings: 8
Cooking Time: 35 Minutes
Ingredients:

- 2 cups jasmine rice, rinsed and drained
- Chicken stock to fill up to line 2
- ¼ cup almonds, chopped
- ½ cup button mushrooms, halved
- 1 shallot, minced
- ½ tablespoon butter

- 1 garlic clove, minced

Directions:

1. Add the rice to your Hamilton Beach Rice Cooker.
2. Melt butter in a small pan over medium heat. Stir in shallots and cook for 2 minutes. Add in mushrooms and cook for 1 minute more, then remove from heat.
3. Transfer the sautéed ingredients and the chopped almonds into the rice cooker. Fill the inner pot with broth up to line 2. Stir and close the lid.
4. Press the WHITE RICE button and let the cooking cycle complete.
5. Once the cooker switches to WARM mode, let the rice sit for 10 minutes.
6. Fluff the rice and transfer to serving bowls.

Nutrition Info: Calories: 198 Fat: 3g Carbohydrates: 38g Protein: 3g

68. Vegetables Rice

Servings: 6
Cooking Time: 35 -40 Minutes
Ingredients:

- 2 tablespoons unsalted butter
- ¼ cup carrots, sliced in rounds
- 1 ½ cups long-grain white rice
- 2 cups vegetable stock
- 1 tablespoon fresh Italian parsley, chopped
- 1 teaspoon dried thyme
- ¼ cup frozen peas
- 1 tablespoon chopped almonds

Directions:

1. Take a small skillet and place it over medium heat.
2. Melt 1 tablespoon of butter and add carrots, stirring occasionally for 2-3 minutes.

3. In the meantime, add rice to your Hamilton Beach cooker.
4. Stir in stock, thyme, parsley, peas and the sautéed carrots.
5. Close the lid and cook on WHITE RICE mode.
6. Once the cooking cycle is over, the cooker will switch to WARM mode.
7. Let it sit for 10 minutes, then carefully open the lid.
8. Fluff the rice and stir in 1 tablespoon of butter and almonds.
9. Serve immediately.

Nutrition Info: Calories: 212 Fat: 5g Carbohydrates: 32g Protein: 15g

69. Exciting Shrimp And Quail Eggs With Java Rice

Servings: 4
Cooking Time: 40 Minutes
Ingredients:

- 12 whole quail eggs, raw
- ¼ cup fresh leeks, minced, for garnish
- For Rice
- 2 cups mushrooms
- 2 cups uncooked white rice, rinsed
- 1 cup frozen peas, thawed
- 1 cup frozen shrimps, unthawed
- ¼ teaspoon fish sauce
- 1 pinch of black pepper and salt
- Water
- 2 tablespoons butter
- Ice bath (2 parts water + 1 parts ice cube)
- Garnish
- ¼ cup fresh parsley, minced
- 1 teaspoon toasted garlic cloves

Directions:

1. Add quail eggs in a steam tray.
2. Add all the ingredients, except the eggs and butter, to your Hamilton Beach Cooker. Pour water to line 4 and place the steam tray on top.

3. Close the lid, push the WHITE RICE button, let the cooking cycle complete.
4. Once the Hamilton Beach Cooker switches to WARM mode, open the lid.
5. Transfer the steamed eggs to an ice bath and soak them.
6. Pat them dry with paper towels and peel the skin, cut them in halves lengthwise.
7. Fold in butter in your rice and season to taste.
8. Serve with a eggs on top and garnish with leeks.

Nutrition Info: Calories: 497 Fat: 23g Carbohydrates: 59g Protein: 36g

70. Bacon Mushroom Risotto

Servings: 6
Cooking Time: 30-40 Minutes

Ingredients:

- 2 teaspoons olive oil
- 2 Portobello mushrooms, sliced into 1 inch pieces
- Salt and pepper to taste
- 2 garlic cloves, minced
- 4 ½ cups vegetable broth
- 2 ½ cups white wine
- 1 cup Arborio rice
- 1 pinch of dried basil
- ¼ cup Parmesan cheese, grated
- ¼ cup Romano cheese, grated
- ¼ cup heavy cream
- 6 strips bacon, cooked crispy and crumbled

Directions:

1. Set your Hamilton Beach Cooker to STEAM mode and heat oil for 5 minutes.
2. Add in mushrooms, salt, pepper and stir. Cook until tender, for about 3-4 minutes. Stir in garlic and cook for 1 more minute.
3. Pour 1 cup of broth and ½ cup of white wine. Give it a good stir.

4. Add rice, basil and season with a pinch of salt and pepper.
5. Stir well, close the lid, and cook until the liquid has been absorbed.
6. Carefully open the lid and add another cup of broth and ½ cup of white wine.
7. Keep stirring until the liquid is absorbed again. The whole process should take around 30-40 minutes.
8. Once tender, add cheese and season with salt and pepper again. Stir in bacon and heavy cream, and serve in bowls garnished with more bacon.

Nutrition Info: Calories: 354 Fat: 18g Carbohydrates: 25g Protein: 12g

71. Simple Salmon And Rice Delight

Servings: 6
Cooking Time: 40-45 Minutes
Ingredients:

- 2 salmon fillets
- 2 teaspoons ground ginger
- 3 tablespoons soy sauce
- 1 garlic clove, minced
- 2 teaspoons brown sugar
- ½ teaspoon red pepper flakes
- 1 green onion, sliced
- 2 cups brown rice
- Salt and black pepper to taste

Directions:

1. In a bowl, mix ginger, soy sauce, brown sugar, and chili flakes. Place the fish into the marinade and refrigerate for 30 minutes.
2. Add 2 cups of brown rice to your Hamilton Beach cooker and pour water to line
3. Close the lid, push the WHITE RICE button, and let the cooking cycle complete.
4. In the meantime, take the fish out of the fridge and place it on a steamer basket.

5. After 30 minutes of cooking, carefully open the lid and add the steamer basket with the salmon fillets.
6. Close the lid and let the cooking cycle complete.
7. Once the cycle is over, open the lid and check if the salmon flakes easily with a fork. If not, close and let it cook for a few minutes more.
8. Serve the rice over the salmon and sprinkle with freshly sliced green onion.

Nutrition Info: Calories: 460 Fat: 28g Carbohydrates: 77g Protein: 37g

72. Original Moroccan Brown Rice

Servings: 5
Cooking Time: 45-50 Minutes
Ingredients:

- 1 ½ cups long-grain brown rice
- 2 ¾ cups water
- Salt and pepper to taste
- 1 teaspoon coriander, ground
- ½ teaspoon cardamom, ground
- 3 tablespoons butter, cut in pieces
- ¼ cup preserved lemon, minced for garnish

Directions:

1. Grease the Hamilton Beach cooker with cooking spray. Add rice, water, coriander and cardamom. Season with salt and pepper, and stir gently.
2. Close the lid, press BROWN RICE, and let the cooking cycle complete.
3. When ready, carefully open the lid and stir in butter.
4. Close the lid and let it sit in WARM mode for 10 minutes.
5. After 10 minutes, open the lid, fluff the rice and squeeze lemon. Serve warm.

Nutrition Info: Calories: 423 Fat: 33g Carbohydrates: 41g Protein: 29g

73. Sweet Corn And Wild Rice

Servings: 4
Cooking Time: 25-30 Minutes
Ingredients:

- ¼ cup fresh parsley, minced
- ¼ pound baby carrots, skins scrubbed, tops trimmed
- ¼ pound baby corn on cobs, rinsed
- Pinch kosher salt
- Rice
- 2 cups vegetable broth
- 1 ½ cups uncooked wild rice, rinsed and soaked in 2 cups water for 30 minutes
- 1 cup Green Beans, ends and stringy bits removed, sliced into ½-inch long slivers
- 1 can 15-ounce cannelloni beans
- 1 can 15-ounce diced tomatoes
- 1 can 15-ounce whole kernel sweet corn, rinsed
- Dash black pepper
- Dash kosher salt
- Water

Directions:

1. Place carrots and corn in your steamer tray.
2. Season with salt and set aside.
3. Add all ingredients listed under the rice to your rice cooker and stir.
4. Pour just enough water to reach the level 4 mark.
5. Place steam tray on top.
6. Close the lid, push the BROWN RICE button and let the cooking cycle complete.
7. Once ready, the cooker will automatically switch to WARM mode.
8. Open the lid and drain vegetables.
9. Serve garnished with fresh parsley and a portion steamed veggies

Nutrition Info: Calories: 247 Fat: 11g Carbohydrates: 34g Protein: 7g

74. Dill And Lemon "feta" Rice

Servings: 3
Cooking Time: 45 Minutes
Ingredients:

- 1 ½ cups long-grain white rice
- 2 cups chicken stock
- 2 tablespoons olive oil
- 2 small boiling onions, finely chopped
- ¼ cup pine nuts
- ¼ cup fresh lemon juice
- 1 tablespoon fresh dill, minced
- 1 ½ teaspoons fresh mint, minced
- 1 cup crumbled feta
- 1 lemon, cut in 8 wedges

Directions:

1. Grease your Hamilton Beach Cooker's inner pot with cooking spray. Add the rice and stock.
2. Close the lid, push the WHITE RICE button, and let the cooking cycle complete.
3. Once the cooker switches to WARM, let the rice simmer for 10 minutes.
4. When ready, carefully open the lid.
5. Heat oil in a skillet over medium heat. Stir in onions and cook for 5 minutes.
6. Add in pine nuts and cook until golden; this should take about a minute.
7. Transfer the onions and pine nuts to the rice cooker.
8. Sprinkle with lemon juice, dill and mint, and stir gently.
9. Cover and keep in WARM mode for 10 more minutes. Next, transfer to a serving dish and top with feta and lemon wedges.

Nutrition Info: Calories: 254 Fat: 6g Carbohydrates: 45g Protein: 5g

75. Rice And Chinese Sausage

Servings: 6
Cooking Time: 1 Hour
Ingredients:

- 2 cups medium-grain white rice
- 1 cup Chinese sausage, thinly sliced diagonally
- ½ cup green onions, thinly sliced
- 2 ¾ cups water
- ¼ cup cilantro leaf, garnish
- 2 tablespoons black sesame seeds, to garnish

Directions:

1. Add rice, water, onions and sausage to your Hamilton Beach cooker and stir.
2. Close the lid, push the WHITE RICE button, and let the cooking cycle complete.
3. Once the cooking cycle is over, the cooker will switch to WARM mode.
4. Press STEAM and set timer to 15 minutes.
5. When done, carefully open the lid and fluff the rice.
6. Transfer to a serving dish and garnish with sesame seeds and cilantro.
7. Serve and enjoy.

Nutrition Info: Calories: 196 Fat: 2g Carbohydrates: 39g Protein: 4g

76. Chicken Biryani And Saffron Cream

Servings: 4
Cooking Time: 40 Minutes
Ingredients:

- 1 pound chicken breast
- 1 cup plain yogurt
- 1 ½ teaspoons coriander
- 1 teaspoon turmeric
- ½ teaspoon cumin

- 1 onion, diced
- 1 piece 2-inch fresh ginger, peeled
- 3 garlic cloves, peeled
- 1 jalapeno, stemmed
- 3 tablespoons canola oil
- 1 ½ cups white rice
- 6 cloves garlic
- 1 cinnamon stick
- 3 cups chicken broth
- 1 teaspoon salt
- 1 pinch of saffron mixed with 2 tablespoons of heavy cream
- 3 tablespoons cilantro, chopped
- 3 tablespoons mint, chopped
- 1 lime

Directions:

1. Cut the chicken breast into chunks. Take a bowl and add yogurt and powdered spices, then add the chicken and coat it well. Set aside.
2. In a food processor, puree onion, ginger, garlic and chili pepper. Set aside.
3. Push the STEAM button and set timer to 20 minutes. Pour the oil and heat it.
4. Add in the onion paste and cook until the liquid starts to evaporate and the paste is slightly brown; this should take about 15 minutes.
5. Next, add the rice, whole spices and give it a good stir. Smooth the top and place the marinated chicken pieces on top.
6. Pour broth and season with salt. Close the lid, push the WHITE RICE button, and let the cooking cycle complete.
7. Once the cooker switches to WARM, open the lid and stir in saffron cream and mix.
8. Sprinkle with chopped cilantro and mint. Close the lid again, push the STEAM button and set timer to 5 minutes. Once ready, carefully open the lid, squeeze lime and fluff the rice.
9. Scoop onto a serving platter and garnish with freshly chopped cilantro, cashews, fried onion or raisins.

Nutrition Info: Calories: 585 Fat: 18g Carbohydrates: 3g Protein: 33g

77. Thai Prawn With Peas Fried Rice

Servings: 4-6
Cooking Time: 40 Minutes
Ingredients:

- 2 tablespoons oil
- 1 medium onion, halved and thinly sliced
- 2 garlic cloves, minced
- 1 red hot chili, chopped
- 2 cups brown rice, soaked and drained
- 1 cup raw prawns, peeled and deveined
- Water, to fill up to line 2
- ½ cup canned peas, drained
- 1 tablespoon light soy sauce
- 1 tablespoon fish sauce
- ½ cup loosely packed fresh coriander, chopped
- 4 large whole eggs, beaten
- Hot chili sauce to taste

Directions:

1. Drain the soaked rice for 2 hours prior to cooking. Add water to your inner pot up to line 2. Place the inner pot in the rice cooker and add rice.
2. Give it a good stir and close the lid. Cook on BROWN RICE and allow the cooking cycle to complete.
3. Once done, let the rice sit for 10 minutes and remove the lid. Fluff it and transfer to a bowl. Wash the inner pot and place it back to your cooker.
4. Press BROWN RICE and wait for a few minutes to heat up.
5. Add oil and the beaten eggs, fry until lightly browned. Flip and fry for 1 minute more.
6. Remove the fried eggs from the inner pot and let cool, then chop the eggs into small pieces. Pour 1 tablespoon of oil to the pot and heat.
7. Add garlic and chili and sauté for 1-2 minutes or until fragrant. Stir in the prawns and cook for 2-3 minutes until opaque.

8. Next, stir in peas and rice, and season with salt and pepper. Stir in ¾ parts of coriander and cook for 3 minutes.
9. When ready, remove and serve with eggs, prawns and onion mix. Top the rice with coriander and chili sauce and serve.

Nutrition Info: Calories: 358 Fat: 16g Carbohydrates: 42g Protein: 10g

78. Red Ruby Beans And Rice

Servings: 6
Cooking Time: 25-35 Minutes
Ingredients:

- 1 cup white rice
- 1 ¼ cups water
- 1 ½ teaspoons cumin
- 2 teaspoons salt
- 3 teaspoons chili powder
- 1 ½ teaspoons garlic powder
- ¾ teaspoon paprika
- 1 bell pepper, finely diced
- 1 onion, finely diced
- ½ pound ham, diced
- 1 can red kidney beans, drained and rinsed

Directions:

1. Add rice, water, bell pepper, onions and spices to your Hamilton Beach cooker.
2. Stir and close the lid. Push the WHITE RICE button and start the cooking cycle.
3. After 10 minutes, open the lid, stir in ham and close the lid.
4. Let the cycle finish and wait for the cooker to switch to WARM mode.
5. Open the lid and let it sit for 5-10 minutes.
6. Serve and enjoy!

Nutrition Info: Calories: 328 Fat: 10g Carbohydrates: 23g Protein: 23g

79. Fine Chile Cheese Rice

Servings: 8
Cooking Time: 25-35 Minutes
Ingredients:

- 2 cups white rice
- 3 cups chicken broth
- 1 can (4 ounces) diced green chilies
- ½ medium onion, diced
- 2 teaspoons garlic powder
- 1 cup Monterey Jack Cheese, shredded
- 1 tablespoon butter

Directions:

1. Take a skillet and place it over medium heat.
2. Heat the butter, add in onion and garlic.
3. Sauté until translucent, for 1-2 minutes.
4. Then transfer to your Hamilton Beach cooker, along with rice, chilies and broth.
5. Give it a good stir and close the lid.
6. Cook on WHITE RICE mode until the cooking cycle is over.
7. Once cooked, open the lid and sprinkle with the shredded cheese.
8. Let it sit in WARM mode with the lid closed for 5-7 minutes to melt the cheese. Next, carefully open the lid, stir gently and serve immediately.

Nutrition Info: Calories: 291 Fat: 9g Carbohydrates: 42g Protein: 11g

80. Mesmerizing Garlic And Chicken Fragrant Rice

Servings: 3
Cooking Time: 35-40 Minutes
Ingredients:

- 3 cups uncooked jasmine rice
- 3 cups water
- 2 tablespoons sesame oil

- 2 cubs chicken bouillon
- ½ cup olive oil
- 1 green onion, chopped
- 2 cloves garlic, smashed
- 1 2-inch piece fresh ginger root, crushed
- 1 chicken thigh with skin

Directions:

1. Add the rice, water, chicken bouillon, sesame oil, green onion, garlic and ginger to your Hamilton Beach Cooker. Swirl gently. Place the chicken on thigh on top.
2. Close the lid, push the WHITE RICE button, and let the cooking cycle complete.
3. When done, carefully open the lid and serve immediately.

Nutrition Info: Calories: 423 Fat: 23g Carbohydrates: 15g Protein: 31g

81. Ultimate Orange Chipotle Risotto

Servings: 4
Cooking Time: 35-45 Minutes
Ingredients:

- 1 tablespoon butter
- 1 cup small onion, diced
- 1 cup Arborio rice
- 3 cups hot water
- 1 cup orange juice
- Zest from ½ orange
- 1 teaspoon saffron thread, optional
- 1 chipotle chile in adobo
- 3 ounces asiago cheese + 1/2 cup grated asiago cheese
- ¼ cup freshly chopped parsley

Directions:

1. Set your Hamilton Beach Cooker to STEAM mode and melt butter.

2. Stir in the onions and sauté for 2-3 minutes until translucent.
3. Add the rice, water, orange juice, saffron, zest, chipotle pepper and saffron.
4. Close the lid and cook on BROWN RICE mode until the cooking cycle is over.
5. When the rice cooker switches to warm mode, open the lid and top with freshly grated cheese and herbs.
6. Season with salt and pepper, give it a good stir and serve.

Nutrition Info: Calories: 321 Fat: 9g Carbohydrates: 46g Protein: 13g

82. Mouthwatering Curry Chicken Jambalaya

Servings: 4
Cooking Time: 35-40 Minutes
Ingredients:

- 2 tablespoons oil
- 1 cup onion, chopped
- 1 tablespoon garlic, minced
- 2 tablespoons curry powder
- 2 cups water
- 1 can tomato sauce (8 ounce)
- 1 pack jambalaya mix (8 ounce)
- 1 pound boneless and skinless chicken breast, cut into 1-inch cubes
- ½ cup golden raisins
- ¾ cup plain yogurt
- ⅓ cup chopped cashews

Directions:

1. Heat oil in the Hamilton Beach Rice Cooker on WHITE RICE mode.
2. Stir in the garlic and sauté for 1 minute.
3. Add curry powder and sauté for another minute.
4. Pour in the water, tomato sauce, Jambalaya mix and raisins.
5. Close the lid, push the WHITE RICE button.
6. Let the cooking cycle complete.
7. Once the cooker switches to WARM mode, open the lid and stir in

yogurt.
8. Let it simmer for about 5 minutes.
9. Serve sprinkled with cashews.

Nutrition Info: Calories: 562 Fat: 17g Carbohydrates: 72g Protein: 37g

83. Bacon And Onion Rice

Servings: 3
Cooking Time: 20-30 Minutes
Ingredients:

- 1 ½ cups uncooked white rice
- 3 tablespoons butter
- 4-6 bacon slices
- ½ medium-sized onion

Directions:

1. Cut onion into ½-inch chunks and slice bacon into ¼-inch square pieces.
2. Add the rice to your Hamilton Beach cooker and pour water to line
3. Close the lid and cook on WHITE RICE mode until the cooking cycle completes.
4. Take a medium-sized frying pan and place it over medium heat. Add bacon and fry it until crisp, it should take around 2-3 minutes.
5. Once the rice is ready, carefully open the lid and stir in butter. Add the bacon onion mixture and give it a good stir. Serve hot and enjoy.

Nutrition Info: Calories: 499 Fat: 23g Carbohydrates: 55g Protein: 16g

84. Dirty Rice And Chinese Chorizo

Servings: 4
Cooking Time: 40 Minutes
Ingredients:

- A handful asparagus, thick-stemmed with tough ends snapped f, sliced in halves

- Olive for drizzle
- Sea salt to taste
- For Rice
- 2 pieces, medium Chinese Chorizo, diced
- 2 cups mushrooms broth
- 2 cups white long-grain rice
- 1 cup frozen peas, thawed
- 1 can of 15-oz button mushrooms, stems rinsed and drained
- 1 teaspoon garlic powder
- 1 pinch of black pepper
- 1 pinch of kosher salt
- Water
- Freshly chopped parsley
- Garnish
- ¼ cup fresh parsley, minced
- 1 teaspoon toasted garlic cloves

Directions:

1. Place asparagus in a steam tray and season with salt. Drizzle olive oil on top.
2. Stir in all the ingredients into the rice cooker.
3. Add water up to line 4 and place the steam tray on top.
4. Close the lid, push the WHITE RICE button, and let the cooking cycle complete.
5. Once it goes off, carefully open the lid and remove the steam tray.
6. Drain the asparagus.
7. Serve by ladling 1 portion of rice into a plate.
8. Sprinkle with freshly chopped parsley.
9. Garnish with a portion of asparagus and enjoy.

Nutrition Info: Calories: 498 Fat: 24g Carbohydrates: 54g Protein: 26g

85. Curious Red Rice

Servings: 8
Cooking Time: 65 Minutes
Ingredients:

- 2 cups red rice, rinsed and drained
- Water to fill up to line 2
- Butter for grease
- Salt to taste

Directions:

1. Grease the inner cooking pot with butter.
2. Add rice to your Rice Cooker and season with salt.
3. Fill the cooker with water up to line 2 mark. Swirl and close the lid.
4. Press the BROWN RICE button and let the cooking cycle complete.
5. Once the Hamilton Beach Cooker switches to WARM mode, let the rice sit for 10 minutes.
6. Then, fluff the rice and transfer to serving bowls.

Nutrition Info: Calories: 226 Fat: 3g Carbohydrates: 43g Protein: 6g

86. Shiitake Black Bean Rice

Servings: 6
Cooking Time: 25-35 Minutes
Ingredients:

- 1 cup shiitake button mushroom, diced
- 1 cup long-grain rice
- ½ cup cooked black beans
- 1 red onion, finely chopped
- 3 garlic cloves, minced
- 1 ½ teaspoons olive oil
- 2 tablespoons onion powder
- 2 cups water
- ¾ tablespoon sea salt

Directions:

1. Push the STEAM button and set timer to 5 minutes.
2. Heat the olive oil and stir in the onions.
3. Sauté for 2 minutes until translucent.

4. Add in the garlic and cook for 1 minute until fragrant.
5. Then, add in the remaining ingredients and close the lid.
6. Push the WHITE RICE button and let the cooking cycle complete.
7. Once ready, carefully open the lid and stir well before serving.

Nutrition Info: Calories: 304 Fat: 17g Carbohydrates: 33g Protein: 13g

87. Simplest Tomato Rice

Servings: 5
Cooking Time: 45 Minutes
Ingredients:

- 2 teaspoons olive oil
- 1 tomato, large, stems removed, chopped
- 2 cups white rice, washed
- ⅔ teaspoon salt
- ¼ teaspoon ground black pepper

Directions:

1. Add rice to your Hamilton Beach Cooker and pour water to up to level 2.
2. Stir and remove 5-6 tablespoons of water from the cooker.
3. Add in olive oil, stir in the tomato and season with salt and pepper.
4. Close the lid, push WHITE RICE, and let the cooking cycle complete.
5. Once ready, carefully open the lid and fluff the rice.
6. Serve and enjoy!

Nutrition Info: Calories: 322 Fat: 10g Carbohydrates: 54g Protein: 6g

88. Spicy Cajun Wild Rice

Servings: 6
Cooking Time: 55-65 Minutes
Ingredients:

- 1 cup uncooked wild rice

- 1 can chicken broth (14 ounce)
- ¼ cup water
- ½ pound Andouille sausage, diced
- ½ cup diced sweet onion
- 1 cup chopped fresh mushrooms
- 1 tablespoon garlic, minced
- 1 can (10 ounce) condensed cream mushroom soup

Directions:

1. Add wild rice, chicken broth, sausage, water, mushrooms and garlic to your Hamilton Beach Cooker. Press the STEAM button and set timer to 40 minutes.
2. Wait until the mixture starts to boil, with the lid open, and stir gently.
3. Close the lid and let it cook for the remaining cycle or until the rice is tender.
4. When ready, open the lid and stir in the ream mushroom soup. Serve hot.

Nutrition Info: Calories: 297 Fat: 15g Carbohydrates: 26g Protein: 16g

89. Easy To Make Lime Cilantro Dish

Servings: 4
Cooking Time: 35 Minutes
Ingredients:

- 2 cups of white rice, long-grain washed
- 2 teaspoons olive oil
- 1 lime zest and juice of ½ lime
- 2 tablespoons fresh cilantro, minced
- 1 teaspoon salt

Directions:

1. Take a skillet and place it over medium-low heat.
2. Add rice and oil and stir-fry for 5 minutes.
3. Transfer the toasted rice to your Hamilton Beach Cooker and add

water to level 2 mark.

4. Close the lid, press WHITE RICE and cook until the cooking cycle completes.
5. Once done, open the lid and fluff the rice.
6. Transfer to a serving bowl and add lime juice, zest and cilantro.

Nutrition Info: Calories: 247 Fat: 10g Carbohydrates: 27g Protein: 12g

90. Peanut Rice And Bell Pepper

Servings: 6
Cooking Time: 25 Minutes
Ingredients:

- 3 bell peppers, finely chopped
- 1 cup soaked white rice
- 1 red onion, finely chopped
- ¼ cup peanut butter
- ¼ cup tomato puree
- 1 teaspoon paprika powder
- 1 teaspoon sea salt
- 2 cups water

Directions:

1. Take a bowl and mix in peanut butter and ¼ cup of water, then set aside.
2. Stir in all the other ingredients to your Hamilton Beach Cooker.
3. Pour the peanut butter mix in the cooker. Close the lid, push the WHITE RICE button, and let the cooking cycle complete.
4. Once the pot switches to WARM mode, remove the lid and stir. Serve warm.

Nutrition Info: Calories: 368 Fat: 9g Carbohydrates: 63g Protein: 10g

91. Fragrant Basmati Rice

Servings: 3

Cooking Time: 35-45 Minutes
Ingredients:

- 1 cup basmati rice
- 1 ½ cups water
- ¼ teaspoon salt
- 1 cinnamon stick (4 inches)
- 3 green cardamom pods

Directions:

1. Rinse the rice and drain. Add the listed ingredients and the rice to your Hamilton Beach cooker.
2. Give it a good stir and close the lid. Cook on WHITE RICE mode and allow the cooking cycle to complete.
3. Once it goes off, the cooker will automatically switch to WARM mode.
4. Keep on WARM mode for 15 minutes, lid closed.
5. After 15 minutes, carefully open the lid.
6. Fluff and serve into serving bowls.

Nutrition Info: Calories: 275 Fat: 4g Carbohydrates: 45g Protein: 5g

92. Sweet Ginger Porridge

Servings: 4
Cooking Time: 20-30 Minutes
Ingredients:

- 4 tablespoons honey
- 5 cups filtered water
- 1 cup rice, short grain, washed
- 1 tablespoon ginger, freshly grated
- 1 teaspoon kosher salt

Directions:

1. Wash the rice thoroughly and add it to your Hamilton Beach Cooker.

Season with salt and ginger. Stir well and close the lid.
2. Cook on STEAM mode for 20-25 minutes until the desired consistency is obtained.
3. Once ready, carefully open the lid and stir well.
4. Divide among rice bowls and serve with a drizzle of honey.

Nutrition Info: Calories: 205 Fat: 3g Carbohydrates: 44g Protein: 4g

93. Almonds Corn Quinoa

Servings: 4
Cooking Time: 40-50 Minutes
Ingredients:

- 1 cup quinoa
- 1 carrot, diced
- ½ cup sweet corn
- 8-9 almonds
- 7-8 kale leaves, chopped
- 1 teaspoon salt
- 2 cups water
- 1 teaspoon paprika powder

Directions:

1. Place the quinoa in your Rice Cooker. Add the rest of the ingredients and stir gently.
2. Close the lid, push the BROWN RICE button, and let the cooking cycle complete.
3. Once the cooker switches to WARM mode, let it rest for 5 minutes.
4. Serve with sliced avocado and tempeh (optionally).

Nutrition Info: Calories: 181 Fat: 5g Carbohydrates: 1g Protein: 7g

94. Southwestern Rice Cooker Quinoa Yum

Servings: 5
Cooking Time: 50-60 Minutes

Ingredients:

- 12 ounce boxed quinoa
- 1 can of 10 ounce undrained tomatoes and green chili peppers
- 1 can of 15-oz black beans, rinsed and drained
- ½ a small pack taco seasoning, dry

Directions:

1. Take a bowl and mix in taco seasoning, quinoa, 1 cup of water, tomatoes, pepper and beans. Transfer the mixture to your Hamilton Beach cooker.
2. Close the lid, push the BROWN RICE button, and let the cooking cycle complete. When ready, open the lid, fluff the rice and serve immediately.

Nutrition Info: Calories: 512 Fat: 31g Carbohydrates: 88g Protein: 32g

95. Sensible Mirin Rice

Servings: 2
Cooking Time: 25 Minutes
Ingredients:

- 2 shiitake mushrooms, dried
- Water to reach level 2 mark
- 2 cups medium-grain white rice
- ¾ ounce carrots, peeled
- ⅓ slice fried tofu, chopped in strips
- 1 ounce chicken, cubed
- 1 tablespoon mirin
- 1 tablespoon soy sauce, light
- ¼ teaspoon dashinomoto
- ⅓ teaspoon kosher salt

Directions:

1. Take a bowl and add dashinomoto, mirin, salt, and soy sauce.

2. Soak the tofu in this mix, keep the soup stock for later use. Slice the carrot into strips.
3. Remove hard tips from shiitake mushrooms, slice them into strips.
4. Pour the soup stock to shiitake water and mix.
5. Add the rice to your Hamilton Beach Cooker and pour the already prepared stock.
6. Pour water up to line 2 and stir in the remaining ingredients.
7. Close the lid, select WHITE RICE, and let the cooking cycle complete.
8. Once it goes off, carefully open the lid and fluff the rice. Serve and enjoy!

Nutrition Info: Calories: 459 Fat: 14g Carbohydrates: 50g Protein: 30

96. Toasted Coconut Yellow Rice

Servings: 4
Cooking Time: 25-35 Minutes
Ingredients:

- 2 cups white rice, rinsed
- 1 can (14 ounce) coconut milk
- 1 ¼ cups water
- ¼ cup sweetened flaked coconut
- 1 teaspoon ground turmeric
- ½ teaspoon kosher salt

Directions:

1. Place the rice in the Hamilton Beach cooker.
2. Heat coconut milk, water, half flaked coconut, turmeric and salt in a small pan over medium heat.
3. Cook for 7-10 minutes until the turmeric dissolves and the color is uniform.
4. Transfer the mixture over to the rice cooker.
5. Close the lid, push the WHITE RICE button, and let the cooking cycle complete.
6. In the meantime, toast the remaining coconut flakes for 5 minutes in

a skillet over medium heat.
7. Once the cooker switches to WARM mode, let it sit for 5 minutes.
8. Then, carefully open the lid and fluff the rice.
9. Sprinkle with the toasted coconut and serve.

Nutrition Info: Calories: 382 Fat: 24g Carbohydrates: 56g Protein: 22g

97. Simplest Curry Rice Ever

Servings: 5
Cooking Time: 20 Minutes
Ingredients:

- 2 cups uncooked white rice, rinsed and drained
- 3 cups water
- 3 tablespoons mild curry powder

Directions:

1. Stir in rice, curry powder and water to your Hamilton Beach Cooker.
2. Close the lid, press WHITE RICE, and let the cooking cycle complete.
3. Once the cooker switches to WARM mode, let it sit for 5 minutes. Fluff the rice and enjoy!

Nutrition Info: Calories: 225 Fat: 9g Carbohydrates: 29g Protein: 9g

98. Fuss Free Simple Risotto

Servings: 2-4
Cooking Time: 45 Minutes
Ingredients:

- 1 ½ cups Arborio rice
- 4 ½ cups hot chicken stock
- 1 cup grated parmesan cheese

Directions:

1. Add rice and chicken stock to your Hamilton Beach Cooker.
2. Close the lid, push the BROWN RICE button, and let the cooking cycle complete.
3. Once it goes off, carefully open the lid and fluff the rice.
4. Close the lid and let it on in WARM mode for 10 minutes.
5. Sprinkle parmesan cheese on top, stir and serve immediately.

Nutrition Info: Calories: 485 Fat: 18g Carbohydrates: 67g Protein: 12g

99. Generic Brown Rice

Servings: 8
Cooking Time: 65-75 Minutes
Ingredients:

- 2 cups brown rice, rinsed and drained
- Water to fill up to line 2
- Butter for greasing
- Salt to taste

Directions:

1. Grease the inner pot and add the rice. Season with salt. Fill the inner pot with water up to line 2. Swirl well and close the lid.
2. Cook on BROWN RICE mode until the cycle completes and the rice cooker goes to WARM mode. Let it sit for 10 minutes.
3. Fluff the rice and serve.

Nutrition Info: Calories: 174 Fat: 1g Carbohydrates: 37g Protein: 4g

100. Coconut Rice And Roasted Almonds

Servings: 6
Cooking Time: 25-35 Minutes
Ingredients:

- 1 cup white rice
- 2 cups coconut milk
- ¼ cup shaved coconut

- 8-9 almonds
- ½ teaspoon cardamom powder
- ½ teaspoon sea salt

Directions:

1. Add all the listed ingredients to your Hamilton Beach Cooker, except for the almonds.
2. Close the lid, push the WHITE RICE button, and let the cooking cycle complete.
3. Once the cooker switches to WARM mode, let it sit for 10 minutes.
4. In the meantime, toast the almonds in a skillet over medium heat.
5. Open the lid and add in the toasted almonds.
6. Give it a good stir and serve.

Nutrition Info: Calories: 323 Fat: 7g Carbohydrates: 69g Protein: 10g

Printed in the USA
CPSIA information can be obtained
at www.ICGtesting.com
LVHW040931251123
764901LV00005B/903